Becoming Confederates

EST. 75 1938
YEARS
THE UNIVERSITY OF GEORGIA PRESS 2013

Mercer University Lamar Memorial Lectures No. 54

BECOMING CONFEDERATES

Paths to a New National Loyalty

GARY W. GALLAGHER

THE UNIVERSITY OF GEORGIA PRESS   Athens and London

© 2013 by the University of Georgia Press
Athens, Georgia 30602
www.ugapress.org
All rights reserved
Set in Sabon and Zapatista by Graphic Composition, Inc.
Manufactured by Thomson-Shore, Inc.
The paper in this book meets the guidelines for
permanence and durability of the Committee on
Production Guidelines for Book Longevity of the
Council on Library Resources.

Printed in the United States of America
13 14 15 16 17 P 5 4 3 2 1

Library of Congress Cataloging-in-Publication Data

Gallagher, Gary W.
Becoming Confederates : paths to a new national loyalty / Gary W. Gallagher.
pages cm. — (Mercer University Lamar memorial lectures ; no. 54)
Includes bibliographical references and index.
ISBN 978-0-8203-4496-6 (hardcover : alk. paper) — ISBN 0-8203-4496-6
(hardcover : alk. paper) — ISBN 978-0-8203-4540-6 (pbk. : alk. paper) —
ISBN 0-8203-4540-7 (pbk. : alk. paper)
1. United States—History—Civil War, 1861–1865—Social aspects.
2. United States—History—Civil War, 1861–1865—Causes.
3. Patriotism—Confederate States of America—Case studies.
4. Change of allegiance—United States—Case studies.
5. Lee, Robert E. (Robert Edward), 1807–1870.
6. Ramseur, Stephen Dodson, 1837–1864.
7. Early, Jubal Anderson, 1816–1894. I. Title.
E468.9.G34 2013
973.7′13—dc23
2012046530

British Library Cataloging-in-Publication Data available

⚜

For Peter Onuf and Steve Cushman,
much valued colleagues and dear friends

⚜

Contents

❧

Acknowledgments

❧

I was flattered when Sarah Gardner invited me to deliver the 2011 Lamar Lectures at Mercer University. I have great admiration for many of the Lamar lecturers and have assigned several of the books that grew out of the series in my classes. I consider it a high honor to join this impressive roster of scholars. Preparing the lectures allowed me to develop themes I had identified while working on other projects, and the experience at Mercer proved to be delightful. I am much indebted to Sarah and the other members of the Lamar Lectures committee—Nancy Anderson, David A. Davis, John Thomas Scott, and Douglas Thompson—as well as to Bobbie Shipley, who oversaw myriad details relating to my visit. They all helped make my turn as the Lamar lecturer both productive and pleasurable.

Books that emerge from the Lamar Lectures carry the imprint of the University of Georgia Press, a fact that set me up for a very pleasant publishing experience. Managing Editor Jon Davies oversaw my manuscript from the beginning, taking care to make the process as expeditious and efficient as possible. Beth Snead also helped at various points, and Debora R. Holmes did a fine job as copy editor. I am indebted to all of them.

Several colleagues helped at various stages of this project. David Blight is one of them—though he probably would be surprised to know it. I delivered a version of the chapter on Lee at a conference at the Huntington Library, and David's comments after the talk persuaded me that a short book on the topic of loyalty to the Confederacy might be worthwhile. Caroline E. Janney read all the chapters and offered her typically astute comments, many of which sharpened my arguments. Elizabeth R. Varon also read the entire text and raised questions I otherwise would have overlooked. Her work on Robert E. Lee has been very helpful to me. Stephen B. Cushman brought his gift for language and sharp eye for analytical and structural inconsistencies to the task of critiquing my chapters. Finally, Joan Waugh gently prodded me to rethink aspects of the manuscript, both substantive and stylistic. I have come to rely heavily on her insightful responses to everything I write and consider nothing finished until she has weighed in. David, Carrie, Liz, Steve, and Joan reminded me yet again of how much generosity exists in the field of Civil War studies.

The dedication acknowledges my good fortune in having Peter Onuf and Steve Cushman as colleagues at the University of Virginia. They have made me a better scholar and teacher and brought an ample measure of humor and comradeship into my life—for all of which I am most grateful.

Becoming Confederates

Introduction

The seeds of this short book lie in my examination of Stephen Dodson Ramseur as a case study in the development of officers in the Army of Northern Virginia. I undertook that military biography more than thirty years ago, tracing the young North Carolinian's rise from lieutenant to major general in just more than three years. In the course of reading Ramseur's voluminous correspondence, I was impressed with the intensity of his commitment to the Confederacy. Following graduation from West Point and less than a year in the U.S. Army, he resigned well before his home state of North Carolina seceded, behavior that contrasted sharply with Robert E. Lee's well-known struggle to chart a path during the secession crisis. Turning his back on the United States seemed an easy choice for Ramseur, and his willingness to do so despite uncertainty about North Carolina's political course struck me as notable. His conception of loyalty permitted an easy transition from one national identity to another, which, I thought, must have been true of other southern officers as well. With Ramseur and Lee in mind, I thought it might be worth revisiting the subject of loyalty at some point.[1]

My work on Ramseur came at a time when scholars were debating fundamental questions relating to the Confederacy. The slaveholding republic lasted just four years but has cast a large shadow over a good part of U.S. history. Its stormy trajectory witnessed massive human and material loss, the end of the institution of slavery, and the development of a stream of historical memory that retained force for many decades after Lee's soldiers stacked arms at Appomattox in April 1865. Yet many historians have questioned whether the Confederacy was really a nation at all, arguing that its white population never developed true feelings of national loyalty.

That model surely did not fit Ramseur, I knew, and probably not Lee either.[2]

Reading and research over the next two decades have persuaded me of four things that help frame the chapters of this book. First, I believe the Confederacy was a nation. I consider references to a war between the North and the South to be fundamentally flawed because four southern states—Kentucky, Missouri, Maryland, and Delaware—never left the Union, and a big section of the most important slaveholding state broke away to form West Virginia in the midst of war. It is most accurate to think of the conflict as a contest between two mid-nineteenth-century nation-states—the United States versus the Confederacy. One of the two nations, whose entire history unfolded against a background of all-encompassing warfare, simply did not last very long.

My second belief is that a substantial majority of the Confederacy's white residents developed a strong national identity. Only these people should be called Confederates. I oppose the terms "northerner" and "southerner" to describe the opposing populations. The term "southerner" embraces all white and black residents of the fifteen slaveholding states in 1860, millions of whom, including the overwhelming majority of African Americans, would not have considered themselves Confederates. Among white residents of the eleven Confederate states, however, support for the nation ran deep, although establishing exact percentages of those who supported or opposed the Confederacy—or those who merely sought to remain aloof and unharmed until fighting ceased—is impossible. Despite undeniable evidence of substantial internal opposition to Jefferson Davis's administration and the war, one fact stands out: only a citizenry determined to achieve independence would have waged a conflict lasting four years, killing one in four of their white military-age males, and inflicting widespread economic and social dislocation.[3]

My third framing observation is that mainline military forces represented the most important institutional expression of the Confederate nation. Composed of regiments with strong state identifications, the national armies—and, most important, Lee's Army of Northern Virginia—provided tangible and highly visible proof of a collective identity that both united and transcended region, state, and locality. Well before the war's midpoint, Lee and his army functioned much as George Washington and the Continental Army had during the American Revolution. Lee became easily the most important Confederate leader, and hopes for success rested ever more heavily on the campaigns he and his soldiers waged. As a Confederate officer observed in early 1864, "General Robt. E. Lee is regarded by his army as nearest approaching the character of the great & good Washington than any man living. He is the only man living in whom they would unreservedly trust all power for the preservation of their independence." A Georgia woman put it more succinctly, describing Lee as "that star of light before which even Washington's glory pales."[4]

My final observation, which led directly to my choice of topic for this book, is that military officers formed an important component in the equation of Confederate loyalty. Their statements and conduct not only influenced the men they led but also helped shape attitudes and expectations on the home front. Their reasons for embracing the Confederacy help illuminate the larger topic of Confederate identity and shed light as well on the complex web of loyalties that contended for supremacy during the turbulent sectional squabbling of the late antebellum years.[5]

I take my analytical cue from David M. Potter, who belongs on any short list of the most perceptive interpreters of mid-nineteenth-century U.S. history. In an essay titled "The Historian's Use of Nationalism and Vice Versa," Potter usefully reminds readers that every human being possesses numerous overlapping and often mutually reinforcing loyalties, with different ones emerging as most important at various times. Potter discusses, among other things, cultural factors, "the invigorating effect which war has had upon national spirit," and "community of interest, not in the narrow sense of economic advantage only, but in the broad sense of welfare and security through membership in the society." Within the South during the Civil War era, the last of these applied most obviously to white insistence on maintaining supremacy in a society that included millions of enslaved black people. Potter also alludes to the tendency among some historians to deny nationality to groups of whom they morally disapprove, even when a group may in every sense satisfy the "theoretical criteria of nationality." Confederates and their slaveholding republic long have invited such moral disapproval.[6]

I selected three officers in the Army of Northern Virginia to pursue questions regarding Confederate loyalty. Because his letters first piqued my interest in the topic, Dodson Ramseur was an obvious choice. So was Robert E. Lee. By far the most important figure in the army, Lee traditionally has been presented as a Virginian, a reluctant convert to the Confederacy whose most powerful identification always remained with his home state. My reading of his wartime correspondence in connection with other projects contradicts that image. My third subject, Jubal A. Early, combined elements of Lee's and Ramseur's reactions to the secession crisis—a Unionist who grudgingly accepted Virginia's departure from the United States but later came to personify defiant Confederate nationalism. I had studied each of them from various angles in my previous work, so I brought familiarity with pertinent sources to this project. They do not stand in for all Confederates—no three individuals could do that—or even for all officers in Lee's army. They do represent types of responses to the secession crisis and establishment of the Confederacy that hold interpretive value beyond their specific examples. As a trio, they help us understand the malleability of loyalty and why the war dragged on for four years and achieved such intensity.

At the time of Abraham Lincoln's election, Lee was a fifty-three-year-old lieutenant colonel in the U.S. Army, Early a forty-four-year-old lawyer in Rocky Mount, Virginia, and Ramseur a twenty-three-year-old second lieutenant in the U.S. Army. All were members of the slaveholding class from the Upper South (though none owned many slaves) and graduates of West Point. Lee and Ramseur were devout Christians, Episcopalian and Presbyterian, respectively, whose faith showed in correspondence with their wives, families, and friends. A lifelong bachelor, Early fathered four children with a white mistress in Rocky Mount, cursed often and imaginatively, and gave little serious attention to his personal religion.[7]

I focus on four levels of loyalty for each man—to home state, to the United States, to the slaveholding South, and to the Confederacy. I understand that multiple factors contributed to each of these loyalties, including, but not limited to, importance of family, place, politics, and religion. I sketch in broad strokes and seek to answer one principal question: How did each man define himself at critical points? For example, did Lee's identity as a Virginian predominate when he resigned his commission in the U.S. Army? Was the well-being of the United States most important to him when he supported James Buchanan for president in 1856? Did he continue to think first of Virginia when serving as a Confederate general? Ramseur also supported Buchanan in 1856, but was it because he cared most about the nation or the slaveholding South? And did Early have his home state or the United States most firmly in mind when he opposed secession as a member of the Virginia State Convention in the winter and spring of 1861? The answers to such questions allow us to chart the ebb and flow and interconnections of the various levels of loyalty.

This is not a book about honor or religion, though I accord some attention to both. All three men often spoke of honor and duty, attributing their actions to one or both without feeling the need to define what they meant. The two words possess complex meaning, and the southern concept of honor has inspired a fairly large literature that is beyond the scope of my exploration of loyalty. It is enough to say that for Lee and Ramseur and Early, one definition would not suffice. I will generalize to this extent: when referring to honor or duty—sometimes specifically linked to patriotism—they had in mind how their actions would be perceived by, and reflect on, family and friends and how their public reputations would be affected. As for religion, Lee and Ramseur likely would have placed it first among priorities in their lives, and both believed God's hand ordered all events and that all Christians must strive to be worthy of his approbation. Yet religious considerations did not prompt Lee to leave the U.S. Army or persuade Ramseur to support the Confederacy, and Early, I think it safe to say, never consulted the Bible when facing a moment of decision.[8]

The word "identity" appears often in the pages that follow, but not in the way anyone interested in identity studies would approve. I avoid those often opaque theoretical thickets altogether. When I allude to Lee's Virginia identity, I have in mind his loyalty to home state. Ramseur's Confederate identity, in my formulation, represents his conception of belonging to a national community that promised to safeguard the culture and interests he most prized. Similarly, Early's identity as a loyal citizen of the United States rested on the belief that, under the Constitution, his political and property rights would be protected.

A few themes emerged from looking at my three subjects. First, generational differences mattered a great deal. Born in 1807, Lee lived for many years when sectional tensions garnered few headlines and slavery was seldom a toxic issue. Nine years younger than Lee, Early also grew to maturity before the strident sectionalism of the 1840s and 1850s. In contrast, Ramseur never knew a time free of concern that the white South and its slave-based social system were under attack from the North. The three men's reactions to secession reflected their generational backgrounds, with Ramseur much less inclined to think the best of northerners and more firmly wedded to the slaveholding South than to the United States.[9] Second, in each man's case, the war dramatically increased antipathy toward Yankees. Although hardly surprising, this phenomenon had immense importance in two respects—it produced a more committed effort to win independence and rendered genuine postwar reconciliation extremely unlikely.[10] Third, the examples of Lee, Ramseur, and Early undercut the notion that the doctrine of state rights held sway in the Confederacy. All three thoroughly embraced a nationalist point of view and demanded that state and local interests give way to the needs of the central state.

The last theme relates to the centrality of slavery and race to the loyalties of all three men. Whether looking to state or region or either of the two nations, they often stressed the need to preserve the social and economic structure that guaranteed white control over millions of black people and their labor. Early most often mentioned the economic side of the subject, largely because his father lived close to Ohio, where the prospect of slaves escaping to free territory was higher than in areas farther south. The threat of forced emancipation, whether triggered by John Brown's raid on Harpers Ferry, Abraham Lincoln's proclamation of emancipation, or the movement of U.S. armies into the Confederate hinterlands, raised the specter of potentially bloody social chaos. Even Lee, though typically cast as more moderate in his views on slavery and race than the majority of white southerners, lashed out at anyone who menaced the slave-based social structure. The words of Lee and Ramseur and Early point inescapably to the conclusion that, as historian U. B. Phillips famously observed, "the central theme of Southern history" for the white South always had been "a common resolve indomitably maintained—that it shall be and remain a white man's country."[11]

The white man's country most familiar to Robert E. Lee, Stephen Dodson Ramseur, and Jubal A. Early rested on a foundation of slavery. Ramseur never knew any other, and Lee and Early accommodated themselves to a world without slavery and with less certain white dominance only because the U.S. victory in a great war left them no alternative. In the end, their journeys toward Confederate loyalty and unwavering service in pursuit of independence left them angry and disoriented, bereft of stability in an uncertain world.

CHAPTER ONE

Conduct Must Conform to the New Order of Things

R. E. Lee and the Question of Loyalty

Robert E. Lee should not be understood as a figure defined primarily by his Virginia identity. As with almost all his fellow American citizens, he manifested a range of loyalties during the late antebellum and wartime years. Without question devoted to his home state, where his family had loomed large in politics and social position since the colonial era, he also possessed deep attachments to the United States, to the white slaveholding South, and to the Confederacy—levels of loyalty that became more prominent, receded, or intertwined at various points. Lee's commitment to the Confederate nation dominated his actions and thinking during the most famous and important period of his life.

A letter from Lee to former Confederate general P. G. T. Beauregard in October 1865 provides an excellent starting point to examine his conception of loyalty. Just six months after he surrendered the Army of Northern Virginia at Appomattox, Lee explained why he had requested a pardon from President Andrew Johnson. "True patriotism sometimes requires of men to act exactly contrary, at one period, to that which it does at another," stated Lee, "and the motive which impels them—the desire to do right—is precisely the same. The circumstances which govern their actions change; and their conduct must conform to the new order of things." As so often was the case, Lee looked to his primary hero, George Washington, as an example: "At one time he fought against the French under

Braddock, in the service of the King of Great Britain; at another, he fought with the French at Yorktown, under the orders of the Continental Congress of America, against him."[1] Although he did not say so explicitly, Lee's "desire to do right" surely stemmed from his understanding of duty and honor. That understanding placed him in the uniforms of the United States, the state of Virginia, and the Confederacy within a period of a few weeks in 1861.

Lee's complex loyalties too often get lost in both scholarly and popular assessments. Few historical figures are as closely associated with their native state. His decision to resign from the U.S. Army and cast his lot with Virginia has inspired intensive discussion. The issue typically is framed in binary terms: Was he, above all, a loyal Virginian or an American? Charles Francis Adams Jr. stands among a large group of authors and other commentators who, over the past century and a half, have stressed Lee's identity as a Virginian. A Union veteran of the Army of the Potomac whose ancestors had labored alongside Lee's in forging the nation, Adams addressed the subject in a lecture titled "Shall Cromwell have a Statue?" Speaking to the Phi Beta Kappa fraternity at the University of Chicago in 1902, Adams presented Lee as a man firmly moored to the Old Dominion. "Of him it might, and in justice must, be said," averred Adams, "that he was more than of the essence, he was of the very quintessence of Virginia. In his case, the roots and fibres struck down and spread wide in the soil, making him of it a part." Five years later, speaking at Washington and Lee University, Adams made his point even more strongly: "[T]he child's education begins about two hundred and fifty years before it is born; and it is quite impossible to separate any man—least of all, perhaps, a full-blooded Virginian—from his prenatal traditions and living environment. . . . Robert E. Lee was the embodiment of those conditions, the creature of that environment,—a Virginian of Virginians."[2]

The most influential writer on the topic of Lee's Virginia identity has been Douglas Southall Freeman, whose Pulitzer Prize–winning *R. E. Lee: A Biography* remains by far the fullest reckoning of its subject's life. A proud Virginian himself, Freeman described Lee's decision to resign from the U.S. Army in a chapter titled "The Answer

He Was Born to Make." "The rapid approach of war," wrote Freeman, "had quickly and inexorably revealed which were the deepest loyalties of his soul." Anyone seeking to understand Lee, believed the biographer, need know only that Virginia always remained paramount in his thinking. Freeman reproduced the entire text of Lee's letter to General-in-Chief Winfield Scott, dated April 20, 1861, that announced his resignation and included one of the most frequently quoted sentences Lee ever penned or spoke: "Save in the defense of my native State, I never desire again to draw my sword."[3]

This idea that Lee's Virginia identity, as displayed during the secession crisis, holds the key to understanding his life and career retains great vitality. A few examples will illustrate this phenomenon. Terry L. Jones's *The American Civil War*, a massive volume published in 2010, observes that "[a]lthough he loved the Union and opposed secession, Lee's greatest loyalty was to Virginia." David Goldfield's *America Aflame: How the Civil War Created a Nation*, which appeared a year after Jones's book, takes the same tack. "His fealty to his native state of Virginia," writes Goldfield, "superseded his loyalty to the Union." The most widely read single volume on the war, James M. McPherson's *Battle Cry of Freedom*, similarly describes Lee's decision to leave federal service after Virginia's secession as "foreordained by birth and blood." A literature critical of Lee's generalship that developed between the 1970s and the 1990s likewise stressed the importance of Virginia. Thomas L. Connelly, prominent among those who questioned Lee's contributions to the Confederate military effort, portrayed a man unable to look past the borders of his home state and thus blind to the conflict's larger strategic landscape. "His concept of the war effort was almost totally identified with Virginia," claims Connelly, "and he felt that other theaters were secondary to the eastern front."[4]

Lee the parochial Virginian also appears in the realm of popular culture. Two films directed by Ron Maxwell include scenes that highlight the importance of Virginia to Lee's actions and attitudes. In *Gettysburg*, an adaptation, released in 1993, of Michael Shaara's novel *The Killer Angels*, Lee and his lieutenant James Longstreet discuss their loyalties on the morning of July 2, 1863. Longstreet remarks that his lie with home state and family, a sentiment with which Lee concurs. Neither manifests a significant attachment to the Confederate nation. In *Gods and Generals*, which appeared a decade after *Gettysburg*, Lee makes the same point in a scene just prior to the battle of Fredericksburg. "There is something that these Yankees do not understand, will never understand," comments Lee while gazing across the Rappahannock River toward Ferry Farm, where George Washington had lived. "You see these rivers and valleys and streams, fields, even towns?" he asks with rising emotion. "They are just markings on a map to those people in the War Office in Washington," but for Lee and Confederates they are birthplaces, burial grounds, and battlefields where their ancestors fought: "They are the incarnation of all our memories and all that we are, all that we are." Director Maxwell explained his interpretation of Lee, as well as of Thomas J. "Stonewall" Jackson, succinctly: "Virginia was their home. They would fight for their home."[5]

Although it illuminates only part of the whole story, Lee's loyalty to Virginia certainly predominated during the momentous spring of 1861. It is useful to chronicle, in abbreviated fashion, his road to resignation from the U.S. Army. Stationed in Texas in early 1861, Lt. Col. Lee watched the Union he had served for more than thirty years drift toward disaster. The election of Abraham Lincoln had triggered South Carolina's secession on December 20, 1860. In rapid order, six other states of the Deep South followed suit, including Texas, which departed from the Union on February 1. Shortly after Texas seceded, Lee received orders from Brig. Gen. David Twiggs, who had replaced him in December as head of the Department of Texas, to report to Winfield Scott in Washington. After a sad parting with friends in San Antonio, he began the long journey home, reaching Arlington on March 1.[6]

The national crisis deepened soon after Lee's return to Virginia. Jefferson Davis headed a new Confederate government in Montgomery, Alabama, and tensions escalated regarding the fate of Fort Sumter in Charleston Harbor. In early March, Lee met privately for several hours with Gen. Scott, an interview during which the senior commander likely urged his former staff officer to remain in the U.S. Army. Lee's promotion to colonel of the First U.S. Cavalry Regiment followed on March 16. In the meantime, Confederate secretary of war Leroy Pope Walker offered Lee a brigadier general's commission in the Confederate army. Walker's letter, dated March 15, reached Lee after word of the promotion to head the First Cavalry. Lee apparently did not respond to Walker's letter, but on March 30 he accepted the colonelcy and assignment to command the First Cavalry.[7]

The final storm broke in mid-April. Confederates fired on Fort Sumter on the twelfth, the federal garrison formally capitulated on the fourteenth, and Lincoln issued a call on the fifteenth for seventy-five thousand volunteers to suppress the rebellion. On April 17, Lee received requests to meet separately with Francis Preston Blair Sr., the patriarch of a famous Democratic family well known to Lee, and Winfield Scott. The meetings took place on the morning of the eighteenth. Empowered by Lincoln to "ascertain Lee's intentions and feelings" and by Secretary of War Simon Cameron to make an offer to the Virginian, Blair asked Lee to assume command of the army being raised to put down the rebellion. Among several arguments he deployed, Blair said Scott was too old to take the field and observed that the people of the United States looked to Lee as a "representative of the Washington family"—an allusion to Lee's marriage to Mary Anna Randolph Custis, the daughter of George Washington's step-grandson. Lee, who thought Blair very "wily and keen," declined the offer and proceeded immediately to Scott's office, where he recounted his conversation with Blair and reiterated that he would not accept the proffered command. Tradition has it that Scott, a fellow Virginian, replied, "Lee, you have made the greatest mistake of your life; but I feared it would be so."[8]

Powerful emotions must have pulled at Lee as he pondered his future that evening and the next day. Word of Virginia's secession appeared in local newspapers on April 19, and in the early morning hours of April 20 he composed a one-sentence letter of resignation to Cameron. Later that day Lee wrote a much longer letter to Gen. Scott, the penultimate sentence of which contained the already quoted statement with regard to raising his sword only in defense of Virginia.[9]

The War Department took five days to process Lee's resignation, which became official on April 25. By then he had received an offer from Governor John Letcher to take command of all Virginia's military forces. The fifty-four-year-old Lee traveled to Richmond on April 22, checked into the Spotswood Hotel, and then made his way to the capitol. There he talked with Letcher, who explained that discussions within the state convention had resulted in a recommendation that Lee be given charge of Virginia's troops. Letcher already had dispatched a courier with the offer; that man was en route to Arlington as Lee made his way to Richmond. Lee accepted his native state's call, and Letcher immediately sent his name forward for confirmation—accompanied by a brief text explaining that Lee had resigned his U.S. commission before learning that a major generalcy would be in the offing from Virginia.[10]

On the morning of April 23, Lee set up headquarters and wrote his first order, denominated General Orders No. 1. It stated simply: "In obedience to orders from his excellency John Letcher, governor of the State, Maj. Gen. Robert E. Lee assumes command of the military and naval forces of Virginia." A four-man delegation soon arrived from the convention to accompany Lee to the capitol. Shortly after noon, the five men entered the building, where the delegates were in private session. As he waited for a few minutes outside the closed room, Lee doubtless contemplated French sculptor Jean-Antoine Houdon's life-size statue of George Washington—his model of military and republican virtue. Walking into a crowded chamber, Lee drew the attention of an audience that included notables such as Confederate vice president Alexander H. Stephens, oceanographer Matthew Fontaine Maury, and Superintendent Frances H. Smith of the Virginia Military Institute. The welcoming remarks came from John Janney of Loudoun County, a former Whig and the convention's president. Like Lee and a majority of the delegates to the convention, Janney had opposed secession until Lincoln's call for seventy-five thousand volunteers.[11]

Janney offered effusive praise of the new major general, recounting his service in Mexico and situating him alongside earlier Virginia heroes. The vote for Lee had been unanimous, observed Janney, who then summoned the memory of "Light-Horse Harry" Lee's famous tribute to Washington: "We pray God most fervently that you may so conduct the operations committed to your charge, that it will soon be said of you, that you are 'first in peace,' and when that time comes you will have earned the still prouder distinction of being 'first in the hearts of your countrymen.'" The glowing tribute probably made Lee uncomfortable, especially the suggestion that he might become the Confederacy's Washington. None in the chamber really could have imagined what we now know to be the truth, that four years of cruel war would raise Lee to a position in the Confederacy very like that of Washington during the American Revolution. After Janney finished, Lee offered a three-sentence acceptance, closing with this: "I devote myself to the service of my native State, in whose behalf alone will I ever again draw my sword."[12]

Lee the Virginian indisputably held center stage during the momentous weeks in early 1861. Letters to family members underscored this fact. As he put it to his sister Anne Lee Marshall, "I have not been able to make up my mind to raise my hand against my relatives, my children, my home." Many members of Lee's extended family were staunch Unionists, including his sister Anne and many cousins, several of whom fought for the United States during the ensuing conflict. Some relatives never again spoke to Lee after he left U.S. service. Within his own household, Mary Anna Custis Lee and most of their children harbored Unionist sympathies. Only one daughter, Mary, fully embraced her father's decision to resign from the army. Moreover, approximately one-third of all Virginians who had graduated from West Point remained loyal to the United States. Among the six Virginian colonels in U.S. service in the winter of 1861, only Lee resigned his commission. In short, many Virginians, including some very close to Lee, did not consider the severing of long-held ties to the United States to be their only realistic option during the secession crisis.[13]

Very strong ties to the United States—the second of Lee's four loyalties under consideration—certainly complicated his decision on April 20. Indeed, much in his background pointed toward a different "Answer He Was Born to Make." As already noted, George Washington, the greatest of all Virginians, was Lee's idol, and the Revolutionary general and first president had been a consistent advocate of a national point of view. There would be no nation without Washington, no regular army, no sense of the whole transcending state and local concerns. Lee came from a family of Federalists who believed in a strong nation as well as the need to look after Virginia's interests. In 1798, his father had opposed the Virginia and Kentucky Resolutions, with their strong advocacy for state power, because they would have denied the national government "the means of preserving itself." The Virginia Resolutions, Light-Horse Harry Lee argued, "inspired hostility, and squinted at disunion." If states could encourage citizens to disobey federal laws, "insurrection would be the consequence."[14]

Lee's devotion to the American republic made sense for one who had served it as a gifted engineer, a staff officer who contributed substantively to American victory in the war with Mexico, and a superintendent of the U.S. Military Academy at West Point. He identified the country's professional soldiers, and most especially graduates of West Point, as impartial national servants whose labors amid dangerous circumstances highlighted the shallowness of petty political bickering. Correspondence with his brother Carter in February and March 1848 sheds light on this point. Lee expressed unhappiness with wrangling between President James K. Polk and his Whig opponents over terms of peace in the wake of Winfield Scott's remarkable campaign from Veracruz to Mexico City—a feat of arms made possible, said Lee in seconding Scott's view, only by the actions of officers trained at West Point. "There are many that cry 'Hurra for Clay' & 'hurra for Polk,' & how few that raise their voice for their country," he wrote from the Mexican capital city. Quarrels between Polk and Scott, the latter a Whig whose rumored presidential ambitions irritated the commander in chief, created a situation in which "the Service & perhaps the Country" would have much to lose. "The latter is always first in my thoughts & efforts," affirmed Lee in language his hero Washington would have approved, "& the feelings & interests of individuals should be sacrificed to its good. But it is difficult to get men to act on this principle."[15]

Although Whiggish or even Federalist in his political views, Lee applauded news of Democrat James Buchanan's election in 1856 as best for the nation. "I am anxiously looking for some arrival to give us the result of the late Presidential election," he wrote Mrs. Lee from Fort Brown, Texas, in mid-November, adding that he "saw no hope of Mr. Fillmores election, & though I do not fear Mr Fremont's, I am anxious to see that Mr Buchanans is certain, & that the Union & Constitution is triumphant." Definitive word still had not reached the far corners of Texas a month later. Yet Lee, limited to scanning "plenty of papers here, but all of old dates," allowed himself a tentative optimism. "Mr Buchanan it appears," he wrote, "is to be our next President. I hope he will be able to extinguish fanaticism North & South, & cultivate love for the country & Union, & restore harmony between the different sections." Earlier that year, Lee had spent a hot and uncomfortable Fourth of July along one of the branches of the Brazos River in Texas. In a political atmosphere of swelling sectional turmoil, he chose to emphasize his devotion to the United States in a letter to Mary Lee relating his frame of mind on the anniversary of the nation's birth. "[M]y feelings for my country were as ardent, my faith in her future as true, & my hopes for her advancement as unabated," he assured her on August 4, "as if felt in more propitious circumstances."[16]

Lee opposed secession during the winter of 1860–61, and in the already quoted letter to Anne Marshall described his "devotion to the Union" and "feeling of loyalty and duty of an American citizen." His letter to Winfield Scott on April 20 further testified to how wrenching it had been, in his words, to "separate myself from a Service to which I have divoted all the best years of my life, & all the ability I possessed." Earlier that year, Lee echoed his Federalist father in telling Rooney, his middle son, that the framers meant for the Union to be perpetual. They envisioned "establishment of a government, not a compact, which can only be dissolved by revolution or the consent of all the people in convention assembled. It is idle to talk of secession." Lee recently had been reading Edward Everett's *The Life of George Washington*, published in 1860, and he thought his professional model's "spirit would be grieved could he see the wreck of his mighty labors!" He lamented the possibility that Washington's "noble deeds [would] be destroyed and that his precious advice and virtuous example so soon forgotten by his countrymen."[17]

Despite his clear affection for the United States, Lee left its army—which brings us to a third level of loyalty. He strongly identified with the slaveholding South, and this loyalty, which aligned nicely with his sense of being a Virginian, helped guide him in the secession crisis. In letters and comments addressing his decision to resign from the army, he often mentioned the South as well as Virginia. His political philosophy stood strikingly at odds with the virulent rhetoric of secessionist fire-eaters; however, as he wrote to Rooney well before his resignation, "The South, in my opinion, has been aggrieved by the acts of the North as you say. I feel the aggression, and am willing to take every proper step for redress." In his meetings with Francis Preston Blair and Winfield Scott on April 18, 1861, Lee proclaimed that although he was opposed to secession, he "would not take up arms against the South" or fellow southerners.[18]

A desire to maintain racial control figured most prominently in Lee's southern identity. Often portrayed as opposed to slavery, he in fact accepted the peculiar institution as the best means for ordering relations between the races and resented northerners who attacked the motives and character of slaveholders and seemed willing, or even eager, to disrupt racial stability in the southern states. In late December 1856, he ruminated at considerable length to his wife on the topic. "[S]lavery as an institution," he wrote in contradiction of those such as John C. Calhoun and George Fitzhugh, who trumpeted it as a positive good, "is a moral and political evil in any country. It is useless to expiate on its disadvantages." He also believed slavery "a greater evil to the white than to the black race, & while my feelings are strongly enlisted in behalf of the latter, my sympathies are more strongly for the former." The fate of enslaved millions should be left in God's hands: "Their emancipation will sooner result from the mild & melting influence of Christianity, than the storms & tempests of fiery controversy."[19]

Lee unequivocally denounced abolitionists, alluding to what he termed "the systematic & progressive efforts of certain people of the North, to interfere with & change the domestic institutions of the South." Such actions "can only be accomplished by *them* through the agency of a civil & servile war." Abolitionists might create an apocalyptic moment by persevering in their "evil course." Resorting to a geographical stereotype of New Englanders widely held by white southerners, Lee asked rhetorically, "Is it not strange that the descendants of those pilgrim fathers who crossed the Atlantic to preserve their own freedom of opinion, have always proved themselves intolerant of the spiritual liberty of others."[20]

In October 1859 Lee confronted John Brown, the northern abolitionist most terrifying to the white South, at Harpers Ferry, Virginia. Sent from Washington with a force of Marines, he directed a brief but intense action that resulted in Brown's capture. Two months later, in a letter to Adj. Gen. Samuel Cooper, Lee characterized Brown's raid on the U.S. armory as an "invasion . . . by a band of armed conspirators." The specter of racial conflict, as well as transgressions against constitutional order, stood out in this letter, which also revealed how Lee's loyalties to Virginia, the slaveholding South, and the United States conjoined. Bent on "invading the state of Virginia and exciting rebellion in the South," Brown had been "captured in open resistance to the authority and troops of the Government, and in the perpetuation of treason." Lee had confiscated the raiders' weapons "as rightfully as if taken from any other enemy of the Country."[21]

Unlike many white southerners, including Dodson Ramseur (as the next chapter shows), Lee never used "northerner" and "abolitionist" as synonyms—although sometimes, as in his letter to Mrs. Lee from December 1856, he relegated New Englanders to a problematical category. Extensive intercourse with officers from the North during his long pre–Civil War career in the army probably promoted geographical tolerance. As a young engineer, he had served under Connecticut-born Andrew Talcott, whose high character impressed Lee and laid the groundwork for a long friendship. In Mexico, he showed no inclination to applaud the efforts of northern comrades any less than those from the South. After Mexico City fell, for example, he wrote warmly of Lt. Calvin Benjamin, a New Yorker, and Capt. Simon Henry Drum, a Pennsylvanian, artillerists who were killed in assaults against the Mexican capital. "They were noble fellows," thought Lee, "& after fighting their way like lions each with a gun, into the very batteries at the Tacubya gate, were cut down. . . . Drum in the delirium of death calling to his men, 'forward.' "[22]

But Lee certainly resented northerners who would tamper with the South's racial order, an attitude that continued during the war. Although seldom quoted by historians, his response to Lincoln's final proclamation of emancipation leaves no doubt about the depth of his feeling. On January 10, 1863, he wrote to Confederate secretary of war James A. Seddon, calling for greater mobilization of human and material resources in the face of U.S. military power that threatened complete social disruption in the Confederacy. Lincoln's proclamation laid out "a savage and brutal policy," stated Lee with simmering anger, "which leaves us no alternative but success or degradation worse than death, if we would save the honor of our families from pollution, our social system from destruction." Lee's use of "degradation," "pollution," and "social system"—words often deployed by white southerners in antebellum discussions about the possible consequences of abolitionism—highlight the degree to which Lincoln's policy menaced more than the integrity of the Confederate political state. Although Lee did not single it out, the passage announcing that freedmen "will be received into the armed service of the United States to garrison forts, positions, stations, and other places, and to man vessels of all sorts in said service" must have struck a special chord. It represented nothing less, from a Confederate perspective, than official sanctioning of the type of armed racial conflict that had created widespread anxiety at the time of John Brown's raid.[23]

Two years earlier Lee also had spoken of honor, claiming that "there is no sacrifice I am not ready to make for the preservation of the Union, save that of honour." As a member of the slaveholding aristocracy of Virginia and the South, his sense of honor dictated that he stand with those of his blood, class, and section. Lee hated the idea of disunion but rejected the idea of a country "that can only be maintained by swords and bayonets" and was unwilling to risk forced changes in a social structure predicated on the institution of slavery.[24]

Those who cling to the idea of Lee as preeminently devoted to his state must come to terms with a fourth important loyalty. Once Virginia joined the Confederacy and he exchanged the Old Dominion's uniform for that of the new republic,[25] Lee quickly, and decisively, adopted a national as opposed to a state-centered stance. His most important loyalty during the conflict was to the Confederate nation—something perfectly consistent with his southern and Virginia identities. Lee's national viewpoint stands out vividly in his wartime correspondence. From the opening of the conflict until the final scenes at Appomattox, he urged Confederate soldiers, politicians, and civilians to set aside state and local prejudices in their struggle to win independence. The Confederacy, though born in the Deep South of a secession movement censured by Lee during the winter and spring of 1860–61, maintained a social order he deemed essential for a population counting millions of black people amid the white majority.

Lee articulated his views about the relative importance of state and national concerns on many occasions. A letter to Secretary of State Andrew G. McGrath of South Carolina in late December 1861 provides one example. Just eight months into the war, Lee took the long view regarding the topic of subordinating state to nation. In this instance, he laid out a strong case for mustering South Carolina's "military strength . . . & putting it under the best and most permanent organization. The troops, in my opinion, should be organized for the war." The last sentence addressed the problem of twelve-month volunteers, many thousands of whose enlistments from the spring of 1861 would be ending just as spring military campaigning commenced. Lee preferred "emphatically" that enlistments be for the duration of fighting. Lee warned that George B.

McClellan's Union army near Manassas would hold a huge numerical advantage unless the governments of South Carolina and other states met the national challenge. "The Confederate States have now but one great object in view, the successful issue of war and independence," Lee explained to McGrath: "Everything worth their possessing depends on that. Everything should yield to its accomplishment."[26]

Lee pursued a similar line of argument with Governor Henry T. Clark of North Carolina the following summer. Clark had written about an array of Union "outrages and depredations," to use Lee's language, that had plagued part of the state, requesting additional military protection. Lee responded with a tutorial on the relative importance of committing manpower to national and state purposes. "The safety of the whole State of North Carolina," he asserted from Army of Northern Virginia headquarters, "as well as of Virginia, depends in a measure upon the result of the enemy's efforts in this quarter, which if successful, would make your State the theater of hostilities far more injurious and destructive to your citizens than anything they have yet been called upon to suffer." In other words, the Army of Northern Virginia, waging a defense of the whole nation, acted on behalf of the parts, including North Carolina, and required the maximum resources to carry on its work.[27]

The Confederate people debated a number of issues relating to the expansion of national power at the expense of state authority or individual liberties, and in every instance Lee came down on the side of measures that furthered the nation-building project. Although no precise breakdown of sentiment across the Confederacy in this respect is possible, Lee stood among those most willing to accept greater central power to achieve military victory and independence. Three examples reveal his unflinching Confederate perspective: the implementation of national conscription; the impressment of goods and enslaved labor to support the Confederate war effort; and the arming of slaves as white manpower dwindled.

During the winter and spring of 1861–62, Lee instructed his aide Charles Marshall to "draft a bill for raising an army by the direct agency of the Confederate Government." Lee wanted legislation to extend by two years the service of those who previously had enlisted in good faith for twelve months, to classify all other white males between the ages of eighteen and thirty-five as eligible to be placed into Confederate uniform, and to give Jefferson Davis the power "to call out such parts of the population rendered liable to service by the law, as he might deem proper, and at such times as he saw fit." Marshall aptly noted, "This measure completely reversed the previous military legislation of the South. . . . The efforts of the Government had hitherto been confined to inviting the support of the people. Gen. Lee thought it could more surely rely upon their intelligent obedience, and that it might safely assume command where it had as yet only tried to persuade." Marshall's careful language softened the import of what Lee sought: a Richmond government with the power to compel service from its male citizenry. The U.S. government never had dealt with its male citizens in this fashion (although the Lincoln administration would do so in the spring of 1863), and many Confederate citizens regarded national conscription as a significant abridgement of individual rights and freedoms. Those whose enlistments were extended proved particularly disgruntled, alleging a breach of contract between them and their national government.[28]

Marshall also summarized Lee's ideas about balancing individual rights and state and national authority. Again, the general took a stalwart nationalist stance that departed radically from state rights advocates who accused Jefferson Davis of usurping power in the name of waging an effective war. "He thought that every other consideration should be regarded as subordinate to the great end of the public safety," wrote Marshall, "and that since the whole duty of the nation would be war until independence should be secured, the whole nation should for the time be converted into an army, the producers to feed and the soldiers to fight." Late in 1861, Lee had used virtually identical language and arguments in a letter to Governor John Letcher of Virginia. "The great object of the Confederate States is to bring the war to a successful issue," he insisted: "Every consideration should yield to that; for without it we can hope to enjoy nothing we possess, and nothing that we do possess will be worth enjoying without it."[29]

Lee believed the Confederate government often lagged behind its opponent in adopting necessary measures. In fact, until deep into the twentieth century no administration in American history proved so intrusive into its citizens' lives as that in Richmond during the Civil War. But Lee, who after the war spoke of "the difficulty of a 'Confederate Government' resisting a centralized one," wanted more. He raised this subject with his son Custis, an aide to Jefferson Davis, while the armies lay in winter camps around Fredericksburg in February 1863. "You see the Federal Congress has put the whole power of their country into the hands of their President," he reported with grudging admiration. "Nine hundred millions of dollars & three millions of men. Nothing now can arrest during the present administration the most desolating war that was ever practiced, except a revolution among their people. Nothing can produce a revolution except systematic success on our part." Lee meant military success, which required mobilizing men and matériel on a scale the Confederate government seemed loath to embrace. "What has our Congress done," he asked his son, "to meet the exigency? I may say extremity, in which we are placed!" The politicians had done little, to Lee's way of thinking, although they had "concocted bills to excuse a certain class of men from taking service, & to transfer another class in service, out of active service, where they hope never to do service."[30]

Eleven months later, Lee revisited the problem of obtaining recruits for national service. This time a conflict between the predilections of some Virginians and the needs of the Confederacy occupied his attention. Too many western Virginians enlisted in units "serving near their homes," he wrote Jefferson Davis, a phenomenon encouraged by officers "who are naturally desirous to increase their forces." The enlistees expected to be deployed near where they entered service, which left them far removed from arenas contested by major national armies. "What I have said of Virginia is equally applicable to other States," fumed Lee, who recommended that the "disposition to enlist in organizations somewhat local in their nature and remote from the principal theatres of hostilities should be checked, and the recruits thrown so far as possible into the more important and active armies." The Army of Northern Virginia, which campaigned for the benefit of the entire nation, should take precedence over any local commands: "[A]ll the men that can be obtained should be used to fill up the depleted regiments of this army."[31]

Beyond his unrelenting efforts to find more soldiers, Lee supported the central government's right to impress food, animals, and black laborers. During the winter of 1864, he stated that all the Confederacy's war-related resources should be brought to bear against the enemy. He knew civilians bridled at the loss of crops and other supplies to the Richmond government's impressment agents. This politically charged reality, thought Lee, obliged Congress to enact legislation that apportioned economic burdens fairly. But he nonetheless took a hard line: "I think the present law and orders on the subject should be so modified as to authorize the Government to impress when necessary a certain proportion of everything produced in the country." If leather for shoes could be obtained in no other way, "it should be impressed." And if it required "all the meat in the country to support the army, it should be had." The Confederacy's railroads also should be put to the task of delivering supplies to the military fronts. "I earnestly recommend that no private interests be allowed to interfere with the use of all the facilities for transportation that we possess until the wants of the army are provided for," Lee wrote to the secretary of war. Confederate "railroads should be at once devoted exclusively to this purpose, even should it be found necessary to suspend all private travel for business or pleasure upon them for the present."[32]

Late in the war, Lee supported arming some slaves and freeing all who served honorably in the cause of Confederate independence. He did so not because he harbored secret abolitionist sentiment, as some have argued, but because he believed it necessary to win independence. This recommendation followed his earlier call to substitute black men for white men in noncombatant positions in the armies, thereby freeing the latter to shoulder muskets. "A considerable number could be placed in the ranks by relieving all able bodied white men employed as teamsters, cooks, mechanics, and laborers," he informed Jefferson Davis in the autumn of 1864, "and supplying their places with negroes. . . . It seems to me that we must choose between employing negroes ourselves, and having them employed against us."[33]

Early in 1865, Lee elaborated his thoughts about making soldiers of some slaves in letters to Virginian Andrew Hunter and Congressman Ethelbert Barksdale of Mississippi. Federal military forces continued to penetrate deeper into the Confederacy, liberating slaves as they went. The enemy's "progress will thus add to his numbers," remarked Lee in a hard-eyed assessment, "and at the same time destroy slavery in a manner most pernicious to the welfare of our people. . . . Whatever may be the effect of our employing negro troops, it cannot be as mischievous as this." If the enrollment of some slaves in the army would bring victory, the white people of an independent Confederacy would be left in charge of ordering their social institutions as they saw fit, though admittedly some adjustments would be necessary. If the Confederacy did not use black manpower this way and lost the war, abolitionists of the North would be in charge, slavery destroyed, and the societal convulsions unthinkably wrenching. Lee laid out the stark alternatives for Hunter: "[W]e must decide whether slavery shall be extinguished by our enemies and the slaves used against us, or use them ourselves at the risk of the effects which may be produced upon our social institutions."[34]

Lee's devotion to a slaveholding republic's "social institutions"— he had used the phrase "social system" in his letter to Secretary of War Seddon regarding the Emancipation Proclamation—does much to explain his fierce loyalty to the Confederacy. Union victory, as he told Hunter, would end slavery in a "manner most pernicious to the welfare of our people" and with "evil consequences to both races," by which it is reasonable to infer he meant without a guarantee of white supremacy and with massive economic dislocation. He reiterated to Hunter the opinion expressed to his wife in 1856, namely, that he considered "the relation of master and slave, controlled by humane laws and influenced by Christianity and an enlightened public sentiment, as the best that can exist between the white and black races while intermingled as at present in this country."[35] That relation, which was most desirable in Lee's judgment because it afforded white people control over a huge black population, might be maintained indefinitely if Confederate armies established southern nationality.

Anger at an enemy represented by the Lincoln administration and Union armies in the field deepened Lee's commitment to the Confederacy. This anger contradicts a hoary convention that he harbored no bitterness against his opponents and typically referred to them as simply "those people." "In all his official intercourse and private conversation," claimed one early postwar writer, "Gen. Lee never breathed a vindictive sentiment towards the enemy. . . . He had none of that *Yankee-phobia* common in the Southern army; he spoke of the Northern people without malevolence . . . quite in contrast to the epithets and anathemas which were popularly showered on 'the Yankees.'" The most quoted example of this phenomenon occurred at Antietam, where Lee encountered his youngest son, Rob, an artillerist whose battery had been handled roughly and was moving to the rear. "General, are you going to send us in again?" asked the young Lee. "Yes, my son," replied the general with a smile, "you all must do what you can to help drive these people back."[36]

The idea that Lee exercised restraint in characterizing his enemy collapses in the face of the most cursory reading of pertinent evidence. In 1870, he spoke to William Preston Johnston, son of Confederate army commander Albert Sidney Johnston, about the "vindictiveness and malignity of the Yankees, of which he had no conception before the war." That attitude forms a theme through much of Lee's wartime correspondence and appears frequently in contemporary and retrospective accounts by eyewitnesses.[37]

Long before 1864, the period most often associated with the "total war" carried out by William Tecumseh Sherman and Philip Henry Sheridan in Georgia and the Shenandoah Valley,[38] Lee repeatedly deplored Union actions and policies. His response to the

Emancipation Proclamation, already discussed, was not the earliest example. The conflict's first autumn witnessed the death of Col. John A. Washington, a member of Lee's staff and grandnephew of the Revolutionary hero, at the hands of Union pickets. "His death is a grievous affliction to me," Lee wrote to a cousin, adding, "Our enemy's have stamped their attack upon our rights, with additional infamy & by killing the lineal descendant and representative of him who under the guidance of Almighty God established them & by his virtues rendered our Republic immortal." In December 1861, Lee alluded to "the ruin & pillage" inflicted on various parts of the South by what he termed "the vandals" in blue. Writing to one of his daughters about the fate of Arlington, which had been seized by the U.S. government, he betrayed considerable bitterness. "Your old home, if not destroyed by our enemies," he observed, "has been so desecrated that I cannot bear to think of it. I should have preferred it to have been wiped from the earth . . . rather than to have been degraded by the presence of those who revel in the ill they do for their own selfish purposes."[39]

When Maj. Gen. John Pope arrived in Virginia from the Western Theater in the summer of 1862, he promised a new approach to subduing the Confederacy. In line with congressional Republicans who favored applying harsher policies, Pope announced that he would seize civilian property, hang guerrillas, punish civilians who aided them, and otherwise chastise all Rebels. Pope did not follow through with these threats, but Lee reacted passionately. In late July 1862, he wrote Secretary of War George Wythe Randolph that he hoped to "destroy, the miscreant Pope." (The nineteenth-century meanings of "miscreant," according to the *Oxford English Dictionary*, included "depraved, villainous, base" [adjectives] and "a vile wretch, a villain, rascal" [nouns].) Elsewhere Lee stated that Pope must be "suppressed." Later in 1862, Lee watched from high ground west of the Rappahannock River while Union artillery shelled the city of Fredericksburg as a prelude to heavy fighting two days later. A witness recalled that his chief manifested "a deep melancholy, mingled with exasperation" while looking "fixedly at the flames rising from the city." After staring toward the beleaguered city for some time, Lee said, "These people delight to destroy the weak and those who can make no defence; it just suits them."[40]

Few incidents brought out Lee's bitterness toward the Federals more dramatically than the hanging of his second cousin William Orton Williams as a spy on June 9, 1863. Several years after the event, a letter from Lee to Martha Custis Williams—Williams's sister, whom Lee called Markie—indicated the continuing depth of his feeling. "My own grief . . . is as poignant now as on the day of [the hanging]," he wrote, "& my blood boils at the thought of the atrocious outrage, against every manly & christian sentiment which the Great God alone is able to forgive. I cannot trust my pen to utter my feelings. He alone can give us resignation."[41]

A letter from a clergyman in Culpeper Court House, Virginia, in the summer of 1864 confirmed Lee's low opinion of the Federals. He provided a summary of the letter's contents to Mrs. Lee, who doubtless shared his obvious sense of indignation. The Reverend Martin Cole reported malicious destruction that had left "not a church standing in all that country within the lines formerly occupied by the enemy. All are razed to the ground & the materials used, often for the vilest purposes." Although members of the northern Christian Commission apprised the local commander, Maj. Gen. John Newton, of the outrageous behavior, "he took no steps to rebuke or arrest it." Nothing could be done in the short term, Lee admitted, so "[w]e must suffer patiently to the end, when all things will be made right."[42]

Although Lee thought an enemy who hanged Orton Williams, shelled cities, destroyed churches, and issued presidential edicts calculated to promote racial chaos respected neither the laws of God nor the dictates of decency and honor, he did not view the conflict as a crusade to establish a godly commonwealth. He believed God's guiding hand ordered events but always insisted that humans would decide the outcome of the struggle by fulfilling their duties. Painfully conscious of his own failings, he habitually urged members of his family to strive to be worthy of God's mercy. In May 1863, he replied to his daughter Agnes's wish that the war would end. Were that to happen, he wrote, "What pain & anguish would be turned from many a household! I trust that a merciful God in His own good time will accomplish His holy will & give us peace & happiness. . . . Remember me in your sweet prayers & supplicate the throne of grace for mercy & forgiveness towards me." Shortly thereafter, during the retreat from Gettysburg, he assured his wife, "We are all well & bear our labors & hardships manfully. Our noble men are cheerful & confident. May God in His mercy bless our efforts to serve our country!"[43]

Lee's official correspondence with Jefferson Davis and other political and military leaders did not include many references to God, although orders designed to bolster military morale often connected religion to national purpose. The day after Stonewall Jackson's death, General Orders No. 61 announced to the Army of Northern Virginia that "an all wise Providence" had taken "this great and good soldier" at the height of his powers. "But while we mourn his death, we feel that his spirit still lives," observed the commanding general of the famously pious Jackson, "and will inspire the whole army with his indomitable courage and unshaken confidence in God as our hope and our strength. . . . Let officers and soldiers emulate his invincible determination to do everything in the defense of our beloved country."[44]

A final element in Lee's loyal embrace of the Confederacy rested on his admiration for the soldiers who fought and fell in prodigious numbers under his leadership. The example of Washington and the Continental soldiers cannot be overstated here. During the grim winter encampment at Valley Forge, Washington had bonded powerfully with his suffering men, who, denied adequate supplies by parsimonious state governments and an ineffectual Continental Congress, had maintained an admirable degree of cohesiveness and purpose. "The Commander in Chief again takes occasion to return his warmest thanks to the virtuous officers and soldiery of this Army," wrote Washington, "for that persevering fidelity and zeal which they have uniformly manifested in all their conduct. Their fortitude, not only under the common hardships incident to a military life, but also under the additional sufferings to which the peculiar situation of these States had exposed them, clearly proves them worthy of the enviable privilege of contending for the right of human nature, the freedom and independence of their country." To a significant degree, Washington and his soldiers became synonymous with their fledgling nation as the Revolutionary War ground on, surpassing in importance any political leaders or institutions.[45]

So also did the Army of Northern Virginia, along with its commander, become the most important institutional symbol of the Confederacy, and Lee often reminded his soldiers of their ties to the Confederate nation and to the Revolutionary struggle of their ancestors. In the wake of his victory over McClellan in the Seven Days battles, for example, Lee's congratulatory order to the army lamented the loss of "many brave men" but urged survivors to remember the slain "had died nobly in defence of their country's freedom" and always would be associated "with an event that will live forever in the hearts of a grateful people." The soldiers' "heroic conduct" was "worthy of men engaged in a cause so just and sacred, and deserving a nation's gratitude and praise." The hard winter of 1863–64, when near starvation stalked the camps of the Army of Northern Virginia along the Rapidan River lines, prompted Lee to evoke the suffering and example of Washington's men. He assured the veterans that he had been doing all in his power to feed them properly and hoped the situation would soon improve. The history of the army, he said, "has shown that the country can require no sacrifice too great for its patriotic devotion." Then he compared their travails to those of an earlier generation: "Soldiers! You tread with no unequal step the road by which your fathers marched through suffering, privations, and blood, to independence." If those in the Army of Northern Virginia continued to emulate the Revolutionary generation's self-sacrificing efforts, prophesied Lee, "be assured that the just God who crowned their efforts with success will, in His own good time, send down his blessing upon yours."[46]

Ulysses S. Grant and his armies of blue-clad citizen-soldiers dictated a different end to the conflict, compelling Lee and all other Confederates to confront a profoundly altered postwar world. In General Order No. 9, his April 10, 1865, farewell message to the

Army of Northern Virginia, Lee accorded his highest compliments to men who after "four years of arduous service, marked by unsurpassed courage and fortitude," had "been compelled to yield to overwhelming numbers and resources." Lee's decision to surrender to Grant had arisen from a determination "to avoid the useless sacrifice of those whose past services have endeared them to their countrymen"—those Confederate patriots whose best efforts finally had collapsed in defeat. Lee prayed that a merciful God would extend to all "the brave survivors of so many hard fought battles" his blessings and mercy. He closed with references to the nation—not to the states—for which they had sacrificed and to the personal bond between him and the men: "With an increasing admiration of your constancy and devotion to your country, and a grateful remembrance of your kind and generous considerations for myself, I bid you an affectionate farewell."[47]

Lee's words, though not offered in victory, echoed those of Washington's farewell to the Continental army in November 1783. Both featured allusions to courage, intimidating odds, selfless service to nation rather than to individual states, God's approbation, and personal affection—sometimes in almost identical phrasing. Taking "final leave of those he holds most dear," Washington had "bid them an affectionate—a long farewell," reminding them that the fact that they had attained "the object for which we contended, against so formidable a power, cannot but inspire us with astonishment and gratitude." The soldiers had served the nation, overcoming local attachments and prejudices to "become but one patriotic band of Brothers." Washington hoped "the choicest of Heaven's favors both here and hereafter attend those, who under the divine auspices have secured innumerable blessings for others; With these Wishes, and this benediction, the Commander in Chief is about to retire from service."[48] Thus did Washington, the father of a nation, and Lee, the focal point of a failed Confederate nation, conclude their careers with the armies that meant everything to their respective peoples.

Despite lingering personal grievances against the United States, Lee meticulously refrained from public criticism of the victors while president of Washington College for the remaining five years of his life. Meaningful Confederate loyalty was impossible after Appomattox, and the postwar Lee might best be described as a staunch white southerner and Virginian who officially resumed his prewar fealty to the United States. Duty, he believed, obliged him and all other former Confederates to submit to the dictates of the U.S. government. His attitude toward defeat can be summed up simply. The Confederacy had mounted its best effort, had lost irrevocably on the battlefield to a more powerful foe, and must accept the consequences of that defeat. In statements he knew would be reported, he put aside all impulses to lash out at the North for its conduct during the war or its policies during Reconstruction. This was a painful exercise in restraint because the war had hardened him toward the Confederacy's former enemies.

The Radical Republican political agenda during Reconstruction deepened Lee's animosity. In 1866, he explained to Sir John Acton, who as a Member of Parliament had supported the Confederacy, that he considered it unfair to disenfranchise or otherwise penalize former Confederates if they took the oath of allegiance to the United States. Lee accepted "without reserve the amendment which has already been made to the constitution for the extinction of slavery" but disapproved of congressional legislation or constitutional amendments designed to place black people on a more equal footing with white Americans. He worried that the federal government was assuming too much power and applying it inappropriately to the former Confederate states. If federal power outstripped that of the states by too wide a margin, predicted Lee darkly, the result could be calamitous: "The consolidation of the states into one vast republic, sure to be aggressive abroad and despotic at home, will be the certain precursor of that ruin which has overwhelmed" all similar nations in the past.[49]

Lee knew he was the most prominent ex-Confederate, and from Appomattox through his death in October 1870 he suppressed his bitterness to set an example for the rest of the white South. He was what might be called a situational reconciliationist—someone who said things in public that enhanced progress toward reunion but who never achieved true forgiveness and acceptance vis-à-vis his old enemies. On June 13, 1865, he formally requested a pardon from President Andrew Johnson (no pardon would be granted during his lifetime).[50] Later that summer, he pronounced "it to be the duty of every one to unite in the restoration of the country, and the reestablishment of peace and harmony." He similarly urged Jubal A. Early, who nourished virulent anti-Yankee feelings after Appomattox, to maintain restraint in his writings about the war. "We shall have to be patient and suffer for a while at least," commented Lee to Early regarding northern publications that seemed to treat Confederates ungenerously. "All controversy, . . ." continued Lee, "will only serve to prolong angry and bitter feeling, and postpone the period when reason and charity may resume their sway."[51]

Lee reacted in almost identical fashion in early 1866 when Varina Davis mentioned that Republican politician Schuyler Colfax had made remarks insulting to former Confederates. Lee had not read about Colfax's speech but told Mrs. Davis that he would not have answered it in any case. "*I have thought, from the time of the cessation of hostilities,*" he wrote, "*that silence and patience on the part of the South was the true course,* and I think so still." Controversy would not serve former Confederates well because it would keep animosities near the surface. "These considerations have kept me from replying to accusations made against myself," concluded Lee, "and induced me to recommend the same to others."[52]

Lee completed his time on the stage of nineteenth-century U.S. history without a dominant national identity. Intense private grievances and political scar tissue from the war guaranteed that his renewed loyalty to the United States, compelled by defeat on the battlefield, never could approximate what it had been before the secession crisis. Always the realist, he chose to deal with the present rather than linger on the failed effort to forge a new southern nation. He opposed erecting Confederate monuments because they might alienate the North and add to "the difficulties under which the Southern people labour." His Confederate loyalty, so dominant during the war, did survive when it came to those who had died in uniform. "All I think that can now be done," he counseled one of his former subordinates, "is to aid our noble & generous women in their efforts to protect the graves & mark the last resting places of those who have fallen, & wait for better times." His postwar letters and statements abound with evidence that he thought of himself most often as a Virginian and a white southerner, the antebellum loyalties that had taken him away from the United States and into the Confederacy.[53]

We can never know how often Lee allowed his mind to return to April 23, 1861, when he had entered the capitol in Richmond to accept command of Virginia's forces. Had he thought about George Washington's efforts to forge a national resistance from the efforts of thirteen sometimes obdurate colonies as he walked past Thomas Gibson Crawford's heroic equestrian statue on the capitol grounds, or, a bit later, when he stood beside Houdon's marble effigy outside the chamber where the delegates met? Did he reflect on how his loyalties to Virginia and the slaveholding South had trumped one national loyalty and soon steered him toward another? On that day in Richmond, Lee the Virginian already had begun the change—his loyalties to home state and the South commencing the transmutation into ardent Confederate purpose.

Gen. Robert E. Lee, portrait by photographer Julian Vannerson, probably from March 1864. At the time of this photograph, Lee unquestionably was the most admired public figure in the Confederate nation and just weeks away from his encounter with Ulysses S. Grant in the Overland campaign. Library of Congress, Prints and Photographs Division, reproduction number LC-DIG-cwpb-04402

Thomas Crawford's equestrian statue of George Washington on the
capitol grounds in Richmond, Virginia, photographed in April 1865.
On his way to accept command of Virginia's state forces almost exactly
four years earlier, Robert E. Lee passed the monument featuring
the man he most sought to emulate—and who shaped his loyalties
to Virginia and the United States. Library of Congress, Prints and
Photographs Division, reproduction number LC-DIG-cwpb-02528

Robert E. Lee leaving the McLean House at Appomattox Court House following his surrender to U. S. Grant. A. R. Waud's simple sketch managed to capture a sense of stoic resignation, an attitude evident in Lee's subsequent insistence that former Confederates come to terms with the loss of their nation and focus on the process of reintegration into the United States. Library of Congress, Prints and Photographs Division, reproduction number LC-DIG-ppmsca-21320

Stephen Dodson Ramseur (left) and Frank Huger
in their West Point uniforms on the eve of the
secession crisis. Ramseur and the South Carolina–
born Huger were classmates at the academy, briefly
officers in the U.S. Army, and eager converts to the
Confederate cause. Author's collection

Cover of the sheet music for *Our National Confederate Anthem*. It represents Ramseur's two primary loyalties—to the slaveholding South and the Confederacy—as inextricably linked, while also acknowledging the centrality of soldiers to the national project. Library of Congress, Prints and Photographs Division, reproduction number LC-USZ62-33407

Artist James E. Taylor inaccurately depicted Ramseur
on horseback at the moment of his mortal wounding
at Cedar Creek. Conspicuous bravery in combat resulted
in five wounds for Ramseur, who, like
many other young officers from the slaveholding
class, demonstrated his Confederate loyalty at great
personal risk. Courtesy of the Western Reserve
Historical Society, Cleveland, Ohio

Jubal Anderson Early in Confederate uniform.
Early often affected less formal military dress,
which contributed to his reputation as a colorful
eccentric. Library of Congress, Prints and
Photographs Division, reproduction number
LC-DIG-ds-01484

Front page of *Frank Leslie's Illustrated Newspaper*, November 19, 1859, featuring a portrait of John Brown. Although the accompanying article referred to Brown as "a traitor to the American Union," many northern newspapers were far kinder. Favorable response to Brown and his raid brought a major change in Jubal Early's attitude toward northerners. Library of Congress, Prints and Photographs Division, reproduction number LC-USZ62-137591

"The Ruins of Chambersburg—View of Main Street," an illustration *Harper's Weekly* offered readers three weeks after Early's cavalry burned the Pennsylvania city in retaliation for Federal destruction of civilian property in Virginia. "The burned district covers all the business portion of the town and some of the finest private residences," read Harper's accompanying text. "Bedridden old women even did not elicit any compassion in the breasts of these rebels." *Harper's Weekly*, August 20, 1864

RUINS OF CHAMBERSBURG.—THE MAIN STREET.

"Tracks of the Armies," a propagandistic print by pro-Confederate artist Adalbert Johann Volck, shows a Confederate soldier returning home to find it in ruins and his wife dead in the rubble. Destruction of civilian property by Union troops embittered Lee, Ramseur, and Early, fueling their determination not to succumb to the United States. Author's collection

Contrabands escaping.

Emancipation threatened the slave-based social structure that figured very prominently in the state, southern, and Confederate loyalties of Lee, Ramseur, and Early. In the minds of all three, U.S. armies carried out on a massive scale what John Brown had attempted in October 1859. Edwin Forbes documented the movement of enslaved people to Union lines in this sketch from 1864, on the bottom of which he wrote, "Contrabands Escaping. May 29th Hanover Town Va." Library of Congress, Prints and Photographs Division, reproduction number LC-DIG-ppmsca-2071

J.E.STUARTS GRAVE.

SOLDIERS DIVISION.

"Hollywood Cemetery, Richmond, Virginia—Decorating the Graves of Rebel Soldiers, May 31, 1867." Artist William L. Sheppard, a veteran of Lee's army, sketched one of the primary ways in which white southerners expressed feelings of Confederate loyalty during the postwar years. Leaders and common soldiers each get attention: Jeb Stuart's grave is featured in the upper left and the "Soldiers Division," where most of the Confederate dead from Gettysburg eventually were reinterred, in the upper right. *Harper's Weekly,* August 17, 1867

CHAPTER TWO

He Died as Became a Confederate Soldier

Stephen Dodson Ramseur's Easy Embrace of the Confederacy

Stephen Dodson Ramseur typified a cohort of young men from slaveholding families who made an early and zealous commitment to the idea of a Confederate nation. Reared during the increasing sectional tensions of the 1840s and 1850s, Ramseur developed a powerful sense of southern identity that guided his actions during the secession crisis and into the·war years, more than did concomitant loyalties to his native North Carolina and to the republic he served as a West Point graduate and junior officer in the U.S. Army. Ramseur's unqualified belief in the superiority of a slaveholding society undergirded his southern identity and made for a seamless transition to resolute Confederate purpose. Despite multiple wounds and much hardship during the war, he called for any sacrifice necessary to avoid subjugation to what he deemed a Yankee government and people willing to wage unrestrained war and bent on destroying a social system designed to ensure racial stability and white supremacy.[1]

An outline of Ramseur's brief life will help frame consideration of the interplay among his various loyalties.[2] Born in Lincolnton, at the edge of North Carolina's Piedmont region, on May 31, 1837, he grew up in comfortable circumstances. His father, Jacob A. Ramseur, was a prosperous merchant who owned eight slaves in 1840 and twenty in 1850. Dodson, as he was commonly known to family and friends, attended Davidson College before winning an appointment to West Point, from which he graduated fourteenth of forty-one members in the class of 1860. He served as a captain in the Battalion of Cadets, a post awarded more on the basis of military skills than on academic accomplishment, and later was described by a classmate as "respected, honored, and loved" at the academy.[3] Commissioned brevet second lieutenant upon graduation and assigned to the Third Artillery, he was promoted to second lieutenant of the Fourth Artillery in March 1861.

Ramseur never took up his new assignment. Resigning his commission on April 5, 1861, well before North Carolina seceded, he was commissioned first lieutenant in the Confederate artillery on April 22 and major in the Corps of Artillery and Engineers in the North Carolina State Troops the following month. He commanded a battalion of artillery under Maj. Gen. John Bankhead Magruder on Virginia's Peninsula and saw initial action near Yorktown on April 16, 1862. Ambitious for higher rank, Ramseur left the artillery to become colonel of the Forty-Ninth North Carolina Infantry on April 28, 1862. His principal action with the Forty-Ninth came on July 1, 1862, at Malvern Hill, where he received a serious wound in his right arm during one of the last Confederate attacks on that sanguinary day. Six months of painful convalescence ensued, during which Ramseur received news of his promotion to brigadier general. Recovered by January 1863, he took charge of his brigade, a notable one that comprised the Second, Fourth, Fourteenth, and Thirtieth North Carolina regiments, serving in Brig. Gen. Robert E. Rodes's division of Stonewall Jackson's Second Corps in the Army of Northern Virginia.

Over the next sixteen months, Ramseur fashioned a record as one of the most aggressive and successful brigade commanders in the Confederacy's premier military organization. Throughout his tenure in brigade command, he drilled his soldiers hard, paid scrupulous attention to their logistical needs, and most important, demonstrated initiative and composure in combat—attributes that virtually guaranteed success within the culture of command created and nurtured by Robert E. Lee in the Army of Northern Virginia. The brigade fought doggedly and suffered horrific casualties at

Chancellorsville on May 2–3, 1863. That performance earned Ramseur, who suffered a second wound, praise from both Lee and Jackson. His men helped break the Union line on Seminary Ridge on July 1 at Gettysburg and fought again at the Wilderness on May 6, 1864. Ramseur's finest hour as a brigadier came at Spotsylvania on May 12, 1864, when his soldiers mounted a memorable counterattack after the Union breakthrough in the Mule Shoe salient. Wounded for a third time, he was summoned to army headquarters to receive Lee's personal thanks.

Superior service as a brigadier brought Ramseur assignment on May 27, 1864, to head the division formerly under Lt. Gen. Jubal A. Early, who had been elevated to command of Jackson's old Second Corps. Promoted to major general on June 1, 1864 (the day after his twenty-seventh birthday, making him the youngest West Pointer to achieve that rank in Confederate service), Ramseur acquitted himself well at Cold Harbor and in mid-June accompanied Early and the Second Corps to the Shenandoah Valley. His division led Early's column that saved Lynchburg from a Union force under Maj. Gen. David Hunter on June 17–18 and fought at the battle of the Monocacy on July 9. At Third Winchester on September 19, Ramseur's soldiers overcame initial problems to wage a stubborn defense against imposing odds. Three days later at Fisher's Hill, Ramseur commanded the division of Robert E. Rodes (who had been killed at Third Winchester) in a contest that ended with Confederates abandoning the field in confusion.

Ramseur's growth as a division leader showed at Cedar Creek on October 19. His brigades contributed to stunning Confederate success in the morning, then anchored Early's defense as Federal pressure mounted in the late afternoon. Married since the previous October 28 to his cousin Ellen Richmond, Ramseur had learned three days before the battle of the birth of their only child (a daughter—although he did not know the gender). At Cedar Creek, he wore a flower in his lapel to honor the child and seemed to be infused with tremendous energy. At about five o'clock in the evening, as Ramseur steadied his troops in the face of heavy assaults, a musket ball pierced his right side and punctured both lungs. Captured during a chaotic Confederate retreat and taken to Maj. Gen. Philip H. Sheridan's Union headquarters at Belle Grove, he endured a night of intense pain and died the next morning. On November 3, Federals conveyed the body through the lines near Richmond, where it lay in state at the capitol before transportation several days later for burial in Lincolnton.

Reaction to Ramseur's death bespoke his high reputation within and outside the Army of Northern Virginia. Gen. Lee informed the secretary of war that "the gallant General Ramseur" had been wounded and captured. A Richmond newspaper referred to him as the "Chevalier Bayard" of the Confederacy—a tribute typically bestowed on officers whose service was deemed "without fear and beyond approach"—and the *Raleigh Confederate* reported "his loss to our cause as a melancholy fact." The chief artillerist in Early's Army of the Valley used more prosaic language to make the same point. "Poor Ramseur is dead," he wrote on October 26, 1864, ". . . He was one of the bravest of the brave. He thought himself mortally wounded, sent his watch & messages to his wife." Brig. Gen. Bryan Grimes, a North Carolinian who had served as one of Ramseur's brigade commanders and succeeded him as head of the division, described his "brave and heroic" former superior's death as a loss "to his State and the country at large. No truer or nobler spirit has been sacrificed in this . . . war."[4]

Grimes's allusion to state and nation opens the way to examine Ramseur's various loyalties, and North Carolina is the place to begin. Although the Ramseur family had been far less prominent in the history of the Old North State than had the Lees in Virginia, it nonetheless claimed substantial roots in Carolina soil. The first members arrived from southern Pennsylvania with other German settlers in 1750,[5] and subsequent generations established themselves in the area beyond the Catawba River and eventually in Lincolnton. Active in the Presbyterian church and educational endeavors, the extended Ramseur family included supporters of the Whigs and Democrats in the 1830s and 1840s. Lucy Mayfield Dodson, Ramseur's mother, hailed from Milton, situated in a rich tobacco-growing region just across the state line from Danville, Virginia, and was the daughter of Stephen Dodson, a prominent citizen who served several terms in the North Carolina legislature. Ramseur thus spent his childhood and adolescence among Lincolnton's and Milton's slaveholding elites, secure in his social position among the people in one long-established and another more recently populated part of North Carolina.

Although Ramseur always thought of himself as a North Carolinian and evinced a good deal of state pride, his surviving correspondence includes relatively little evidence that state loyalty stood paramount among factors shaping his life and crucial decisions. In the autumn of 1855, he alluded to North Carolina in explaining what motivated him to do well at West Point. "All that is noble and manly," he began in answering a letter from his mother, "the devoted love that I have for my Parents, the respect that I feel for my friends, the duty that I owe to my old native State, and my own interest and happiness, excite me to continued exertion, to overcome every opposing difficulty and to perform my whole duty. Thus I will *graduate*, and *be a man*, a good and useful man. Then I hope to be qualified for my occupation or profession." Only one other letter from West Point includes a comparable mention of North Carolina. In the autumn of 1856, Ramseur celebrated the election of Democrat Thomas Bragg to the governorship, offering "[t]hree cheers for Gov Bragg, and *nine* for the Gallant old State, which knows so well how to appreciate and reward true merit." Bragg's success demonstrated that he stood "'[f]irst in the hearts' of the people of North Carolina, for such a reward I would gladly live, labor and die."[6]

Ramseur's principal interest in the state seems to have been focused on politics. A devoted Democrat, he followed contests for North Carolina and national offices closely. In August 1855, more than a year before cheering Bragg's reelection as governor, he welcomed the success of Burton Craige, a Democratic member of the House of Representatives who had supported his admission to West Point. "Huzza a thousand times for the gallant Craige and the Democracy of the 7th Congressional District of N.C.," he wrote to his close friend and later brother-in-law David Schenck: "Give me an account of the election at my old Home. Send me the vote of the State if it is convenient." Apart from such examples of engagement with North Carolina politics, Ramseur seldom discussed events in the state unless directly related to his family.[7]

The final stage of the sectional crisis and the war years revealed the degree to which Ramseur looked beyond North Carolina for his primary allegiances. As already noted, he believed North Carolinians waited too long to secede, resigning his U.S. Army commission several weeks before the state's secession convention voted on May 20, 1861, to depart from the Union. As the war unfolded, Ramseur applauded evidence of staunch service by military units from his home state but worried about the degree to which North Carolinians on the home front embraced the Confederacy. As early as September 7, 1861, scarcely 3½ months after North Carolina seceded, he commented about reports of waning enthusiasm behind the lines. "I confess," he wrote in response to a pessimistic report from his brother, "it gives me the 'Blues' to have such a gloomy account from North Carolina. 'A weak, timid governor surrounded by broken down politicians.' With 'few arms and ammunition scarce' surely this is discouraging. That we must all suffer, and severely, I doubt not, but should we therefore hesitate or turn back? A noble spirit spurns difficulties. A victory without dangers is too cheap to be glorious!" Closing his discussion of North Carolina with a tone of hollow optimism, Ramseur professed assurance "that the patriotism and gallantry of the Old North State will now shine forth with increased brilliancy."[8]

The peace faction that developed in North Carolina in 1863–64 profoundly disturbed Ramseur, and the actions of William Woods Holden of Wake County, who edited the *North Carolina Standard* and became the state's most prominent critic of the Davis administration, provoked violent denunciations from him. In the summer of 1863, Ramseur blamed Holden for increased desertion among North Carolina troops in the aftermath of Gettysburg and questioned the depth of support for the war among the state's civilians. "The Army, I think, I know, is *sound*," he wrote his brother somewhat defensively, "and will do honor to the State. If the people at home do not condemn us in dying in this cause." Ramseur's own brigade almost unanimously denounced "Holden & his Tory party," but he wondered, in a passage that revealed obvious doubts, whether it could "be possible that Holden's influence is as potent for *evil* as you think? I can not think so. Are there not true men enough to put him down?"[9]

In February 1864, along the Rapidan River military frontier, Ramseur reacted to news that Holden might enter the gubernatorial race against Zebulon B. Vance. "I have heard it said that Holden will be a candidate for nex[t] Gov.," he observed. "Surely this can not be. If indeed he does run, will not Vance beat him badly." Adopting much more pointed language, he expressed a hope that "North Carolina is not so *low, so disloyal,* as to bow to Holden as Gov. If so, then Good bye to the Old State, whose history might be so high, proud & glorious, but whose fair fame has been tarnished by the blackest of all traitors. But I wont allow myself to think of such a possibility." Although voters inside and outside the army overwhelmingly supported Vance in the election late that summer, Ramseur's overall correspondence relating to Holden leaves no doubt that he harbored continuing concerns about strength of will among North Carolina's civilians.[10]

Stalwart North Carolinians in the Army of Northern Virginia provided Ramseur's greatest source of state identification during the war. After the battle of Ream's Station on August 25, 1864, for example, he cheered Lt. Gen. A. P. Hill's success against Maj. Gen. Winfield Scott Hancock's Union Second Corps and emphasized that victory was due to "*Three North Carolina Brigades*! Hurrah for the Old North State! I hope Richmond papers will do our gallant troops full credit for their glorious achievement." As the last sentiment suggests, Ramseur fretted that Virginia newspapers would slight North Carolina's military contributions. His state pride often took the form of a rivalry with Virginia, whose officers dominated the Confederate high command and whose soldiers, believed Ramseur and many other non-Virginians, garnered unfair attention from the capital city's influential press. He thought his brigade had suffered from such biased reporting after Chancellorsville, where the North

Carolinians had mounted a costly assault—"charged over two, or large parts of two, brigades from Va. who refused to march onward & meet the leaden storm of Yankee bullets." He relied on newspapers in North Carolina to publish the truth about how the state's units performed in battle.[11]

From Ramseur's perspective, his brigade sustained the honor of North Carolina by repeatedly suffering heavy casualties and winning praise from the army's top officers. After his regiments lost more than half their number in savage fighting at Chancellorsville on May 3, 1863, Robert E. Lee sent a plea to Governor Vance for replacements to fill the depleted ranks. "I consider its brigade and regimental commanders as among the best of their respective grades in the army," affirmed Lee in words that residents of any state would welcome regarding their regiments and officers. At Chancellorsville, continued the army's chief, "the brigade was much distinguished and suffered severely, General Ramseur was among those whose conduct was especially commended to my notice by Lieutenant-General Jackson." In his own report of the campaign, Ramseur proudly claimed that his men merited "the thanks of our beautiful and glorious Confederacy."[12]

That claim illuminates how Ramseur ultimately positioned his sense of state loyalty in relation to a more powerful devotion to the Confederacy. On the one hand, disappointment or even shame at his North Carolina connection surfaced at various times. If state politics or antiwar activity hindered an all-out effort to establish a slaveholding republic, as seemed possible in the winter of 1864, Ramseur stood ready to say "[g]ood bye to the Old State." On the other hand, resolute service by North Carolinians in uniform brought out his deepest attachments to the state and its people. Whether assessed in terms of positive or negative behavior, North Carolina's importance, for Dodson Ramseur, always remained secondary to that of the Confederacy.

The United States never inspired an equivalent form of national loyalty during Ramseur's pre–Civil War years. This is not to say he lacked any attachment to his nation. Most important, he drew particular satisfaction from the fact that Americans could boast of a "glorious birthright, won by their ancestors in the bloody revolution." The young Dodson Ramseur knew that his town and county were named after Maj. Gen. Benjamin Lincoln, a Revolutionary hero who accepted the British surrender at Yorktown. He heard stories about one of his great-grandfathers who had fought in the southern campaigns from 1780 to 1783, a veteran of the battles of King's Mountain, where he was wounded, and Eutaw Springs. Closer to home, he could wander over the ground near Ramsour's Mill, where Loyalist and Patriot militiamen collided in a bitter engagement on June 20, 1780 (another of his great-grandfathers operated the mill at the time of the battle). The Patriot victory demoralized Loyalists in the region and created scars in Lincoln County that anticipated those inflicted by a much greater civil war the next century. For many young men of Dodson Ramseur's generation and locale, aged veterans of the battles in the Carolinas provided a tangible link to the nation's Revolutionary origins.[13]

More personally, Ramseur believed a career as a military officer would yield honorable service to the nation. From early boyhood, he often imagined himself a soldier and loved to read about martial figures he called the "World's renowned Heroes." While still at Davidson College in 1854, he had rhetorically noted to David Schenck, "[W]ho knows but that 'I may write my history with my sword.'" Ramseur manifested an awareness of national obligation shortly after reaching West Point in the summer of 1855: "I am *determined to do my duty*. I am aware . . . of the importance and honor of the position I now occupy, but more especially, of that which I will certainly occupy, if I remain true to God, to my Country, to my Parents, and to myself." While at West Point, he explored the historic sites in the area, including the remnant of Fort Clinton, part of a series of Revolutionary War works. His strongest statement of loyalty to the United States mentioned the fort's picturesque aspect. "From my window," he wrote on April 6, 1857, "I look out . . . upon the white ruins of old Fort Clinton, surrounded by dark Cedars, an eloquent and lasting monument to the throes of that 'Time which tried men's souls.' I love the old Fort; and as I climb around its falling battlements, or grope among its dusty dungeons, my heart swells with grateful, patriotic pride, and I thank God that I am an American."[14]

The reverie triggered by the sight of Fort Clinton suggests a genuine affection for the United States, but Ramseur's occasional expressions of national pride pale in comparison to the depth and emotional power of his identification with the slaveholding South. Within the hierarchy of his pre–Civil War loyalties, devotion to the South stood first. He believed fervently in the superiority of the slaveholding society within which he grew to maturity, responded passionately to what he saw as aggressive moves against the South by abolitionists and other northerners, and foresaw the disruption of the republic along sectional lines long before the secession crisis of 1860–61. This loyalty and that to North Carolina, it scarcely needs to be mentioned, complemented one another very well.

Ramseur's thorough embrace of the South's slaveholding society runs throughout his antebellum correspondence. The presidential election of 1856, which pitted Democrat James Buchanan against the fledgling Republican Party's candidate John C. Frémont, stirred Ramseur's strong sectional identity. Robert E. Lee supported Buchanan because he thought the Pennsylvanian would calm sectional tensions and thus help the Union. Ramseur did so because he thought Buchanan would be best for the South. The canvass played out against a backdrop of violence. Congressman Preston Brooks of South Carolina caned Senator Charles Sumner of Massachusetts on the floor of the Senate, and increasing bloodshed in Kansas Territory, where both pro- and antislavery forces perpetrated outrages, received wide coverage in newspapers. "Yes, a crisis has already arrived," Ramseur wrote in mid-September, "which demands every Southerner to stand forth and battle for his rights, sacred rights, bequeathed by Revolutionary Ancestors, dearer to him than life itself. O God! strengthen the hearts and nerve the arms of every Son of the South and enable them to march forth and maintain their rights with the determination and dignity of Freemen!" For white southerners such as Ramseur, the "massacre" of five proslavery settlers near Pottawatomie Creek in Kansas and other incidents raised the specter of an abolitionist war against the peculiar institution. "Does not your blood boil with indignation," he asked a friend in North Carolina, "as you read of abolition & outrages, cowardice & cruelty now daily enacted in Kansas Territory?"[15]

In the wake of Buchanan's victory in November, Ramseur attacked Frémont and the Republicans and offered a paean to the institution of slavery. "Look at the vote of the North in the late contest," he observed, continuing, "[a]n *overwhelming* majority for a renegade, a cheat and *a liar*, only *because* he declared himself in favor of *abolishing slavery*, the very source of our existence, the *greatest blessing* for both master & slave, that could have been bestowed upon us." Ramseur singled out the results in New Hampshire, a traditionally Democratic state where Frémont received 54 percent of the vote, as "amply sufficient to satisfy any impartial mind that opposition to Southern institutions was the ruling principle. See what strides the rankest Abolitionism is making over the entire North!" He labeled Republicans "defeated Scoundrels, Enemies of their country, their Sod, & themselves. Cheers! Long & loud for those noble & daring patriots who have achieved the glorious victory." The conflation of Republicans and abolitionists, which badly distorted political reality in the free states, allowed Ramseur to play down the possibility of any true sectional rapprochement.[16]

Ramseur unabashedly embraced the idea of secession as an alternative to accepting northern interference with the slaveholding South's social structure. Although happy with Buchanan's election, he saw it as no more than a temporary victory. "Our Country is safe for a *few* years more," he suggested, "& I believe those years to be *very few*. . . . [A]ny man of the smallest observation can plainly see, that the Union of the States cannot exist harmoniously; that there must, & *can & will be a dissolution*, wise, peaceful & equitable, I hope, but *at whatever cost*, it must come." By "country," Ramseur in this instance probably meant the United States, as the subsequent reference to "the Union of the States" suggests; however, by 1856 he also thought in terms of a prospective southern nation. He believed the sections had taken divergent cultural paths that eventually would bring a national disruption. Whether he was correct in positing the development of conflicting cultures—a topic historians have debated endlessly—is beside the point. Ramseur accepted such a schism as reality and acted accordingly. "Our manners, feelings & education is as if we were different Nations," he insisted: "Indeed, everything indicates plainly a separation. Look out for a Stormy time in *1860*. In the mean time the South ought to prepare for the worst. Let her establish armories, collect stores & provide for the most desperate of all calamities—civil war."[17]

In early 1858, with coverage of the turmoil in Kansas Territory prominently in the news, Ramseur took a political stance devoid of any foundational loyalty to the United States. "I am a *Secessionist* out and out," he stated proudly, ". . . in favour of drawing the dividing line from the Atlantic to the Pacific. Let us establish a Southern Union, a glorious confederacy, whose foundation shall be Liberté et Égalité. . . . I have the immortal Calhoun with me for now, the '*Balance of Power*' is, or soon will be, lost to us if Kansas is refused admittance as a slave state. I think the South will be wrong to do anything but withdraw & establish an independent & glorious Nation!" Sectional turbulence had been part of Ramseur's consciousness since his preteen years, and he and others of his generation had experienced no war or other defining event that promoted feelings of national solidarity capable of overcoming sectional biases. Moreover, since Florida and Texas had been admitted to the Union as slaveholding states in 1845, four new free states had been added (Iowa, Wisconsin, California, and Minnesota; Oregon would make a fifth one year later), placing the South at a disadvantage of four senators—which undoubtedly contributed to Ramseur's beleaguered frame of mind.[18]

A harsh view of Yankees permeated Ramseur's thinking and letters, an attitude shared by many of his generation. While at West Point, he forged friendships with a few northern men—Ohio-born George Armstrong Custer and New Yorkers Wesley Merritt and Walter McFarland among them—and conceded the presence of "some few noble spirits among the Northerners." Merritt later described Ramseur as "one of my dearest friends at West Point," and both he and Custer sat with their old West Point comrade during his last painful evening at Belle Grove in October 1864. But in the aggregate, nonsoutherners routinely were the targets of Ramseur's biting criticism, with New Englanders most often in his crosshairs. "Among the Cadets," he observed in the autumn of 1855, "none are called Yankees except those from Mass. N.H. Vt. & several of the New England *states*. With these the southerners do not *associate* and indeed, they are generally kept at a respectable distance by all." In April 1856, he professed a willingness to encourage most of the plebes in the next incoming class but not any "miserable Abolitonist," whom he would treat severely. When Ramseur imagined a new southern nation, he thought that "[t]he first infernal Yankee who shows his face across our line [should] be tarred & feathered for the 1st offence & hung as high as Haman for the second!"[19]

Ramseur described southern men as "far superior to the Yankees in every respect except the habit of close application to studies. They make much better officers than the Yankees. . . . more than two thirds of the Cadet Officers are always Southerners." He became very close to a pair of South Carolinians: Wade Hampton Gibbes, whom he described as a "fine fellow, a real southerner, frank, warm-hearted and generous to a fault," and Frank Huger, a member of one of the state's first families. During 1857 and 1858, clashes among cadets over political issues increased, including one pitting William McCreery of Virginia against James Harrison Wilson of Illinois. Gibbes acted as second for McCreery in a contest that resembled a formal duel. The two young men fought to a draw in front of a large crowd of cadets. Gibbes later clashed with New Yorker Emory Upton, who had attended abolitionist Oberlin College before enrolling at West Point, in one of the academy's most famous sectional confrontations of the prewar years. Ramseur's fondness for Gibbes is noteworthy because many at the academy considered the South Carolinian an extreme secessionist and agitator. Ramseur shared Gibbes's political opinions but escaped being labeled a sectional provocateur.[20]

A family financial crisis deepened Ramseur's animosity toward Yankees. His father suffered a major reverse in 1857–58, falling prey to a cascade of debts that eventually ruined his business. Jacob Ramseur lost both social and economic position, settling for a clerkship at a local cotton factory owned by a brother-in-law. The episode took on a doubly painful character for Dodson Ramseur because the key figure in the debacle was a dishonest northerner. He poured out his frustration in early November 1857. Knowledge that his parents and family had "been robbed of all earthly goods by the damning treatchery of a miserable Yankee, a villain, a liar, a fiend of Hell, a ——, too overcomes me." Should he ever meet the man, vowed Ramseur, "I shall certainly crush him to atoms." Looking toward the future, Ramseur envisioned leaving the army after three years to make enough money as a civil engineer to support his struggling family. According to his closest friend, Ramseur's mother declined precipitately after the financial setbacks, succumbing in November 1859. This cruel blow surely intensified the young officer's loathing of northerners.[21]

The strongest evidence that Ramseur's southern loyalty trumped those to both state and nation came during the spring of 1861. Posted to Washington, D.C., with a battery of light artillery, he resided in the capital as the Union broke apart. On February 28, North Carolina voters rejected a proposal to convene a secession convention. Four days later Abraham Lincoln delivered his first inaugural address, which denied the right of secession, placed the issue of civil war in the hands of white southerners the president called "my dissatisfied fellow-countrymen," and reminded listeners (and later readers) of the "mystic chords of memory" connecting all Americans to the Revolutionary generation's sacrifices in creating the nation. Although we have nothing from Ramseur's pen at this time, he surely was disappointed with North Carolina's lack of action and unmoved by Lincoln's plea for union. Four and one-half years earlier he had lashed out at "[b]lack Republican hell-hounds" as a set of "base black-hearted traitors to the Constitution and *our* Country"—by which he meant the white South's slaveholding country protected by "sacred rights, bequeathed by Revolutionary ancestors." On April 5, more than six weeks before his home state seceded and a week before Confederates fired on Fort Sumter, Ramseur submitted a brief letter of resignation to the U.S. Army. He soon began a journey to the new Confederacy's capital in Montgomery, Alabama, away from an old allegiance and toward a new one.[22]

Ramseur's actions in April 1861 raise the question of whether a nascent southern nation existed before Lincoln's election ignited the secession movement in the lower South. As I noted in the introduction, historians have argued for many years, and with considerable fervor, about the existence of true Confederate national sentiment. The manner in which the Confederacy's white population waged the war, with its crushing human and material toll, and its tenacious commemoration of the conflict during ensuing decades persuade me that such sentiment unquestionably existed. For most of the generation that experienced the conflict, the Confederacy represented their best chance to preserve the economic and social promise of the founding generation—the Revolutionary "sacred rights" to which Ramseur often referred—in the face of growing northern dominance. The right to own slaves and take them anywhere, to order society on that bedrock, and thus to maintain control over millions of enslaved black people while guaranteeing a form of equality for all white people took on profound importance. Those who shared Ramseur's views possessed a loyalty to the South forged amid chronic sectional tensions and characterized by bonds of sympathetic interests across state lines, a shared Revolutionary inheritance, and a belief in common destiny—factors important to any conception of national community. The somewhat nebulous abolitionist threat between the 1830s and the early 1850s turned more ominous in the mid-1850s with the advent and rapid success of the Republican Party, setting the stage for a transition from a nascent southern to an actual Confederate nation.[23]

Ramseur's southern loyalty quickly converted into a Confederate one. In September 1856, he told David Schenck that "an awful crisis is approaching, which will decide whether we shall still advance with rapid strides towards a *perfect state* of civilization, as one great and united people; or, whether we shall be . . . destroyed by civil wars." That letter also referred to Republicans as traitors to "*our* Country." Ramseur's emphases in these passages on a civilization and nation that suited proslavery southerners such as he and Schenck help explain his seamless embrace of the Confederacy. The newly established republic represented an ideal to Ramseur, one impossible for him to imagine if the southern states remained yoked to those above the Potomac and Ohio rivers. Confederate vice president Alexander H. Stephens's "Cornerstone Speech," delivered two weeks before Ramseur resigned from the U.S. Army, delineated themes the North Carolinian would have seconded. The "great truth" of black inferiority and the superiority of a slaveholding society formed the cornerstone of the Confederacy, insisted Stephens. "If, we are true to ourselves, true to our cause, true to our destiny, true to our high mission," Stephens said in closing, "in presenting to the world the highest type of civilization ever exhibited by man— there will be found in our Lexicon no such word as FAIL."[24]

From the first weeks of the war until his mortal wounding at Cedar Creek, Ramseur consistently called for subordination of all personal, state, and local interests, including North Carolina's, to those of the new nation. His antebellum loathing for Yankees deepened into hatred as the war progressed, and he consistently argued that no sacrifice was too great to avoid subjugation to Abraham Lincoln and his Union armies. His daring leadership on many battlefields impressed superiors, inspired men in the ranks, and occasioned positive comment behind the lines. The overall impact young officers from the slaveholding class, such as Ramseur, had on Confederate fortunes cannot be quantified; however, they ranked among the most ardent nationalists, and their words and actions surely strengthened feelings of national community.[25]

Ramseur mirrored Robert E. Lee's support for a more intrusive national government if necessary to win the war. He favored any measure that would put the largest number of men into uniform. "I do hope Congress will pass some sensible laws this session," he affirmed in late 1863, "improving the currency & increasing the army by enrolling every man who has employed a substitute." (Most conscripted men who had hired substitutes eventually were made eligible for the draft.) He lauded Jefferson Davis's call for an extension of conscription and suspension of habeas corpus in early 1864—the latter a presidential action that unhinged strong supporters of state rights—as well as a congressional ban on the importation of luxury goods. When the army faced a severe shortage of food in the winter of 1863–64, he favored a national mobilization of resources almost certain to bring hardship to the home front. "The Army must be fed," he insisted, again in language almost identical to Lee's on the same issue, "even if people at home must go without." Black people as well as white should feel the pinch. At a time when soldiers' rations consisted of 1⅛ pounds of flour and ⅛ to ¼ pound of meat per day, he told his brother that their sister "ought to limit the negroes to ⅛ to ¼ lb. of meat, when they have vegetables. Our whole people should do this & send the surplus to the army."[26]

Ramseur exhibited scant patience with soldiers or civilians who obstructed the war effort. A long letter in March 1862 set an exacting behavioral standard that reappeared frequently in his wartime correspondence. Confederate military failures in North Carolina and Tennessee, he believed, had unmasked disgraceful behavior among some southern officers. Roanoke Island had fallen to Union forces under Maj. Gen. Ambrose E. Burnside in early February because of "cowardly *or* ignorant officers who had the command of *brave* men." Unaware of, or indifferent to, the fact that Roanoke's defenders had faced a far more powerful enemy, Ramseur hyperbolically proposed a merciless penalty: "*Hang* every officer who surrenders! We are fighting for *existence* as well as honour & right, but what were the first without the last!" The manner of Fort Donelson's capitulation similarly outraged him. The two top Confederate officers, Brig. Gens. John B. Floyd and Gideon J. Pillow, had abandoned the garrison, leaving Brig. Gen. Simon B. Buckner to suffer the humiliation of accepting U. S. Grant's terms of "unconditional surrender." Pronouncing Floyd "a scoundrel beyond hope of redemption," Ramseur sputtered, "I tell you had F. & P. possessed *moral* courage there would have been a different result at Donelson."

In this letter, Ramseur also echoed Lee's call for resolution among civilians. Although widespread hardship had yet to reach across much of the Confederate home front, news from North Carolina revealed a divided population insufficiently focused on the vital goal of establishing a new nation. "Let us stop our miserable political squabbles," wrote Ramseur angrily, "& as one man put our shoulders to the wheel, pulling & pushing, working & suffering all things, until our independence is achieved, & whoever baulks or hesitates or disobeys, let him be put out of the way, speedily, surely, eternally." In order to win the war, he would accept consolidation of power in the hands of a dictator if necessary and hang traitors— "as did our forefathers"—and cowards.[27]

The level of mobilization favored by Ramseur subjected Confederate society to extreme stress, resulting in desertion, draft evasion, hoarding of goods, vocal opposition to intrusive governmental interference in the economy, and violence on the home front. The American Revolution had witnessed comparable internal fractures within the colonial population (as the battle of Ramsour's Mill showed), and the Lincoln government also dealt with a storm of controversy relating to emancipation, conscription, suspension of habeas corpus, and other policies. But the Confederacy suffered greater turmoil than the United States because the central government took more drastic actions and contending armies operated almost solely within its boundaries. In the backwash of major campaigns and among the hills and mountains of the Confederate upcountry, irregular units and freebooters preyed on civilians and disrupted the normal patterns of life. Few states endured greater political and social roiling than North Carolina, something Ramseur's correspondence with David Schenck tracked in detail. Remarkably, most Confederates adapted to escalating governmental demands, and the Davis administration managed to sustain a fierce resistance to Union military power despite internal strains.[28]

Ramseur made no special allowances for himself during the war, habitually placing the national cause before personal and family concerns. Although desperate to see Ellen Richmond, his cousin and fiancée, in March 1863, he wrote, "Just now, I feel that I would give everything I possess to be with you my Sweetest Nellie," but "[d]uty calls me away and though sometimes my heart *aches* to be with you, yet I remain here willingly in the service of our Country's glorious cause." Dodson and Ellen were married in October 1863 and spent three months during the ensuing winter together in his brigade's camp near the Rapidan River. She left the first week of April 1864, and constant campaigning after the advent of the Overland campaign prevented a reunion. The separation weighed heavily on Ramseur, made all the worse by continuing financial instability for his family in Lincolnton. Two weeks before his death, Ramseur worried about Nellie's condition as she reached the final stage of pregnancy: "I cant tell you how full of anxiety I am to hear from you. . . . Ah! Me! How I do long to be with you My Beloved Wife. . . . We must bear separation, hardship and danger for the sake of our Country. We must dare and do in the cause of liberty. We must never yield an inch or relax any effort in the defence of our homes or the establishment of our nationality."[29]

Most obviously, Ramseur backed unyielding nationalist rhetoric with utter fearlessness, sometimes bordering on recklessness, on the battlefield. His five wounds—at Malvern Hill, Chancellorsville, Spotsylvania, and two at Cedar Creek—attested to his habit of leading from the front. Such was his reputation in this regard that Frank Huger, a West Point friend and able Confederate artillerist, remarked somewhat drolly after Gettysburg, "Ramseur was not hurt this time." Virtually the entire high command of the Army of Northern Virginia praised Ramseur's bravery in the course of the war, as when, after Chancellorsville, Maj. Gen. A. P. Hill remarked on his "gallant leadership" and Maj. Gen. James E. B. "Jeb" Stuart applauded his "heroic conduct." Jubal Early, Ramseur's superior in the 1864 Shenandoah Valley campaign, spoke of his lieutenant as "a most gallant and energetic officer whom no disaster appalled, but his courage and energy seemed to gain new strength in the midst of confusion and disaster. He fell at his post fighting like a lion at bay." An officer in the Second North Carolina Infantry summarized the effect of his style of leadership, describing Ramseur in 1864 as "universally beloved by every man in his brigade. No braver or better man lives than he is. . . . He fights hard and is very successful. His men like to fight under him."[30]

Neither setbacks on the battlefield nor worsening conditions on the home front weakened Ramseur's commitment to an all-out effort to win Confederate independence. "Sad and grievously disappointed" after Gettysburg, he nonetheless urged Nellie not to "dream for a moment that my confidence in the final success of our cause, the complete and glorious triumph of our arms, has abated one jot or one tittle." Although harboring no illusions about how difficult a path lay ahead, he was "prepared to undergo dangers and hardships and trials to the end. We have yet much to suffer. We will suffer it all bravely and heroically. A glorious and honorable Peace will be our rich and lasting reward." He remained resolute after the unprecedented bloodletting of the Overland campaign and difficult operations in the Shenandoah Valley between May and September 1864. "Whatever course the North pursues *our duty is very plain*," he wrote Nellie from near Winchester. "We must fight this fight out. . . . Too much precious blood has been shed for the maintainance of our rights, too great a gulph has been opened up between us & our foes to allow even the idea of reunion to be entertained. No! No! We can & we must bear & suffer all things rather than give up to Yankees & mercenaries our glorious Birthrights."[31]

The last sentence of his letter to Nellie underscores how Ramseur's resolution, deeply rooted in antebellum devotion to the South's slaveholding society, demanded no compromise with an enemy he saw as committed to destroying everything of value. He regularly deployed the harshest terms when referring to Lincoln and the U.S. armies—the "Northern Tyrant" and his "vandal hordes," as he put it in one letter. Although his reaction to the Emancipation Proclamation is not recorded, it easily can be imagined. Lincoln's proclamation of December 8, 1863, which offered amnesty to most Rebels who would swear an oath of allegiance to the United States and accept emancipation, elicited a sarcastic reaction. "Were you not all amused at old Abe's proclamation," he asked Nellie. "Really he takes it for granted that we are all whipped. I think the Old Abe has much work ahead of him before he can persuade us to accept his terms. Don't you?" The targeting of civilian property by Union soldiers during the 1864 Shenandoah Valley campaign provoked Ramseur, who railed against the "hand of the destroyer": "Truly it does seem sacraligeous to despoil such an Eden-like spot by the cruel ravages of war!" The Yankees "respect neither helpless age nor tender woman. Surely a just God will visit upon such a nation and such an army the just indignation of His terrible wrath!"[32]

Devout Presbyterianism and unflinching Confederate nationalism often comingled in Ramseur's letters. As the Army of Northern Virginia prepared for the spring operations in April 1864, he prayed "most earnestly that Our Heavenly Father will so order all things that our Enemy will be driven back in confusion, that his heart may be changed so that he will be persuaded to let us depart in peace. Oh! I do pray that we may be established as an independent people, a people known and recognized as God's Peculiar People!" He revisited this theme in early September, placing the Confederate struggle in a world context. "Let us pray for peace," he implored Nellie, "[t]hat the *minds* & hearts of our Enemies may be turned from War & that our Heavenly Father will establish us in peace & independence. That we may be a Nation whose God is the Lord! An Example of National Christianity to the Nations of the Earth!"[33]

That September, as Ramseur anticipated postwar life in an independent Confederacy, he turned again to the Revolutionary example. Since boyhood, the exploits of the founding generation had captivated him. Those patriots had risked everything in a contest against Britain's military and economic might. They had created a government that protected the rights and liberties essential to Ramseur's idea of a superior slaveholding civilization. "How proud I will be," he wrote Nellie less than two weeks before the battle of Third Winchester opened the final stage of the 1864 Valley campaign, "to tell *our children* that I fought and helped to win some of the great battles of this Second War of Independence! Wont you My Darling."[34]

Six weeks after his superior penned those lines, Maj. R. R. Hutchinson informed Ellen Ramseur of her husband's death. A member of Ramseur's staff present at Belle Grove, Hutchinson wrote on October 20 that the general's "last thought was of you and of his God, his country and his duty." He wished that he "could once see his wife and little child before he died" but trusted to meet them hereafter. "He died as became a Confederate soldier and a firm believer," read Hutchinson's last words, which convey an important truth about the trajectory of Ramseur's loyalties. He considered himself a North Carolinian and southerner for whom the Confederacy had become paramount. Such loyalty to the Confederate nation among other young officers, as well as among the men they led and inspired, helps explain the length and fury of the Civil War.[35]

CHAPTER THREE

Consistent Conservative

Jubal A. Early's Patriotic Submission

Jubal Anderson Early seemingly defines staunch Confederate national loyalty. As an important general in the Army of Northern Virginia, he participated in nearly all the great battles of the Eastern Theater, became widely known for his anti-Yankee rhetoric, and proved willing to lay a hard hand on northern civilian property. Following the war, he assumed a position in the front rank of Lost Cause controversialists, defending the honor and legitimacy of the Confederacy and insisting that only insurmountable advantages of human and material resources and a predilection for indiscriminate brutality had allowed Union forces to achieve a victory. Yet his prewar Unionism and devotion to the Constitution rendered his decision to support first Virginia and then the Confederacy even more fraught than Robert E. Lee's. The apparent contradiction between the Early who espoused love for the Union as a member of the Virginia State Convention and the one whose unrepentant pro-Confederate invective became legendary after the war suggests one or the other stance might have been less than heartfelt. A close look at how Early navigated though treacherous political shoals from the secession winter of 1861 through the early postwar years proves otherwise.[1]

Two episodes illustrate the difficulty of reconciling Early's professed loyalties. On the evening of April 13, 1861, he spoke at the Virginia convention. The day before, Confederate artillery had forced Maj. Robert Anderson's U.S. garrison at Fort Sumter to surrender, and Early, a longtime Whig, deplored the celebratory tone with which many Virginians received the news. Anderson's father, a veteran of the Continental army, was reared in Kentucky while it still belonged to Virginia, a fact Early emphasized in his passionate speech. The patriots who followed George Washington had "fought for our liberties—yes, sir, had fought for South Carolina," observed Early in a jab at the state that inaugurated the secession movement. Although "the flag of my country has been compelled to give way to another . . . ," he said in reference to the banners of the United States and the Confederacy, "I do not despair of the cause of liberty; I do not despair of the Union. I have an abiding confidence in the devotion of the people of Virginia to the Union of the country. . . . [B]ut I must confess it is a matter of regret to me that any Virginian should be found ready to rejoice to see the dishonor to our flag in the hands of a son of one of Virginia's revolutionary soldiers." Sumter had not furthered the Confederates' cause, insisted Early, but rather had placed a "gulf between them and the people of Virginia. The mass of the people will never be found sanctioning their cause."[2]

Just more than four years later, en route to "voluntary exile rather than submit to the rule of our enemies," Early began writing a memoir of the last year of the conflict. Largely completed by the end of 1865, the narrative excoriated white southerners who had remained loyal to the Union, underscoring Early's powerful identification with the Confederate nation. "There were men born and nurtured in the Southern States, and some of them in my own State," he observed bitterly, "who took sides with our enemies, and aided in desolating and humiliating the land of their own birth, and the graves of their ancestors." They deserved, and would receive, "the deep and bitter execrations" of former Confederates and "the immortality of infamy." As for "all the enemies who have overrun or aided in overrunning my country, there is a wide and impassable gulf between us, in which I see the blood of slaughtered friends, comrades, and countrymen, which all the waters in the firmament above and the seas beneath cannot wash away."[3]

Two elements of Early's political philosophy explain his shifting positions. The first, his self-styled Whiggish conservatism, was grounded in profound respect for the work of the founding generation—and most especially for the Constitution—as well as in a belief that the propertied class should maintain a dominant voice in government. Jacksonian democracy's celebration of the common man held no appeal for Early. He believed the government established by the Constitution protected liberty and the sanctity of private property, allowing Americans, whether above or below Mason and Dixon's Line, to prosper. "Government is the result of a compact," Early declared in 1850, "formed between the individuals composing a body politic, by which each agrees to surrender a portion of his natural rights for the common good. It is from this compact all political power is derived." Just governments "afforded to individuals . . . the enjoyment of what they had acquired, or might acquire, as the labor of their hands or the result of their skill. Take away this security and you destroy the main consideration of the compact, render property insecure and the whole fabric of society will tumble in ruins."[4]

Early most clearly articulated the second element in remarks at the Virginia convention. As a Whig, he had been in the political minority most of his adult life with "no voice in the government of this country for years, and . . . nothing to expect, either in a party or a personal point of view," from the work in Richmond. He desired only "to sustain the Constitution and the Union formed by our fathers." Since he was old enough to vote, the Whigs had elected just two presidents—William Henry Harrison, who died after a month in office, and Zachary Taylor, some of whose policies Early ultimately opposed. The dominant political force during this period had been the Democratic Party, most often associated with Andrew Jackson, a towering presence "with whom . . . I never did agree." But on retiring from office, Jackson had given advice that Early took deeply to heart. The president "warned his countrymen of the danger of slavery agitation, and pointed out to them the remedies which they have in the Union and under the Constitution. He advised them to appeal to the people, and said that when all remedies had failed, it became no less the duty of the public authorities than of the people, to yield a patriotic submission." Because Early believed the national government to be a justly formed one, he always had followed Jackson's recommendation to yield a patriotic submission, even when he disagreed with the ruling party's programs. Secessionists acted outside of this behavioral model, argued Early, who posed two provocative questions to the president of the convention: "Sir, does all honor, all chivalry, consist of resisting the government instituted by our forefathers? Does all heroism consist in rebellion against the constituted authorities of the land?"[5]

Early's personal philosophy had developed in a world of slaveholding privilege. He was born on November 3, 1816, near Rocky Mount in Franklin County, Virginia, to Joab and Ruth Hairston Early. A prominent local citizen, Joab Early served as sheriff of Franklin County, a colonel of militia, and a member of the Virginia legislature. At one time, his holdings included more than one thousand acres in Franklin County, and from the 1830s through the end of the antebellum era he owned several dozen slaves. Ruth Hairston Early was the niece of Samuel Hairston of Pittsylvania County, who owned or managed more than three thousand slaves on several plantations in Virginia and North Carolina. Educated as a youth at the best local schools, Jubal Early entered West Point in 1833 and graduated eighteenth in the class of 1837. "I was not a very exemplary soldier," he later wrote, "and went through the Academy without receiving any appointment as a commissioned or noncommissioned officer in the corps of cadets." Never intending to make the army his permanent career, Early served in Florida against the Seminoles before resigning in 1838. He returned to Rocky Mount, read law, was admitted to the bar in 1840, and practiced in the county until the outbreak of war in 1861.[6]

Events in Texas and Mexico in the 1830s and 1840s revealed elements of Early's political thinking that would resurface during the secession crisis. While a cadet at West Point, he wrote feelingly about the Texas revolution of 1835–36. The Mexican constitution of 1824 resembled that of the United States, with a "*General Government*, and also several state Governments, each of which was as independent as our State Governments are." Americans living in the Mexican state of Texas had taken up their new residences in good faith, but as Early saw it, "Santa Anna . . . usurped the Government, overturned the constitution, and established an almost unbounded despotism over what was once the free states of Mexico." Early asserted that Texans "resisting the Tyranny and barbarous cruelty of an *usurped* government" deserved sympathy from anyone who believed in liberty and the rule of constitutional authority. Santa Anna's actions violated the implicit compact between the central government and American immigrants and sought "to deprive Texas of its free constitution."[7] Twenty-five years later, Early characterized Abraham Lincoln's call for seventy-five thousand volunteers to suppress the rebellion of the seven states that created the Confederacy in much the same way, concluding that all who cherished constitutional rights and liberties had free rein to resist.

The annexation of Texas by the United States in 1845 provoked the nation's first major war in thirty years. Annexation had been hotly contested during the presidential election of 1844, with Senator Henry Clay of Kentucky, the Whig Party's popular standard-bearer, opposing it. Although he voted for Clay, wrote Early in his memoirs, "when war ensued, I felt it to be my duty to sustain the government in that war and to enter the military service if a fitting opportunity offered." Impelled by his sense of patriotic submission, he accepted a commission as major of the First Regiment of Virginia Volunteers. He saw no combat during the war but often commanded the regiment, earning a favorable reputation and becoming known across the state for the rest of the antebellum era as Major Early.[8]

Throughout the antebellum period, Early clung to the Whig Party and what he labeled its conservative doctrines promoting the well-being of the propertied class. Elected as a Whig to the Virginia legislature for the 1841–42 session, he lost his bid for reelection by a wide margin (a candidacy in 1853 also failed). Between 1840 and 1852, Early voted Whig in all presidential canvasses, and in 1856—although the party had ceased to exist as a viable organization—he supported Millard Fillmore as a fusion candidate of the

Know Nothings and the Whigs. At a meeting in July 1856, Early lauded the "principles and conservative patriotism" of Fillmore and the Whigs. During the selection process for the Virginia convention, he was variously deemed a "conservative," a "Union," and a "Union straight out" candidate.[9]

Early's decision to follow Virginia out of the Union and into the Confederacy positioned him to forge a military record of considerable distinction in the Army of Northern Virginia.[10] He stood out as a brigade commander at First Bull Run and was promoted to brigadier general in August 1861. Badly wounded at the battle of Williamsburg on May 5, 1862, he returned to the army to fight at Malvern Hill. A brigade commander in Maj. Gen. Richard S. Ewell's division of Stonewall Jackson's wing of the army at Second Bull Run and Antietam, he led the division for parts of both campaigns and earned plaudits from Jackson and Robert E. Lee. In charge of the division again as a brigadier at Fredericksburg on December 13, 1862, Early helped seal a break in Jackson's line. Advancement to major general in April 1863 rewarded Early's excellent service, but he acidly pronounced the promotion so long overdue "that it looks very much like they were picking up the scraps now."[11]

Lee demonstrated his confidence in Early by assigning him difficult tasks. During the Chancellorsville campaign, for example, Early held the Rappahannock River line at Fredericksburg while most of the army marched west to confront Maj. Gen. Joseph Hooker's flanking force. At Gettysburg, he participated in the successful Confederate assaults on the afternoon of July 1 and advocated a joint attack against Cemetery Hill by the corps of A. P. Hill and Richard S. Ewell that evening. After a stinging reverse at Rappahannock Bridge on November 8, 1863, Early temporarily led the Second Corps during the Mine Run campaign before returning to head his division at the battle of the Wilderness. When illness incapacitated Gen. Hill on May 8, 1864, Lee chose Early, who he thought would "make a fine corps commander,"[12] as temporary chief of the Third Corps during fighting at Spotsylvania. Another brief stint with his division in mid-May preceded permanent assignment on May 27 to command the Second Corps and promotion to lieutenant general four days later.

Poised to commence his most famous operations, Early was respected if not loved as a colorful, blasphemous, and sarcastic officer of demonstrated courage. A soldier described him in 1864 as "one of the greatest curiosities of the war," a man "about six feet high" whose "voice sounds like a cracked Chinese fiddle, and comes from his mouth somewhat in the style of a hardshell Baptist with a long drawl, accompanied with an interpolation of oaths." A volunteer member of Early's staff recorded in October 1863 how little it took to provoke blasphemous language from his chief. Hearing Early exclaim, "Lord Jesus Christ, God Almighty," Peter W. Hairston immediately went to see what was wrong and reported that Early said they "had washed a button off his shirt." Early's soldiers called him "Old Jube" or "Old Jubilee" and appreciated his aggressiveness in combat. Lee displayed both affection and a sense of humor in referring to the younger Early as "my bad old man."[13]

In mid-June 1864, Lee sent Early and the Second Corps to deal with Federal threats to Lynchburg and the Shenandoah Valley. In a whirlwind month, Early turned back Maj. Gen. David Hunter's force at Lynchburg on June 18–19, cleared the Valley of Federals, crossed the Potomac and won the battle of the Monocacy near Frederick, Maryland, on July 9, and menaced Washington. Reinforcements detached from the Army of the Potomac prevented his mounting a serious effort to capture Washington, but he maintained a presence in the lower Valley until mid-September and approved the burning of Chambersburg, Pennsylvania, in late July as retaliation for Union depredations in the Shenandoah Valley. General-in-Chief Ulysses S. Grant reacted by ordering Maj. Gen. Philip H. Sheridan to build an army to crush Confederates in the Shenandoah. Early's Army of the Valley, which numbered fewer than 15,000, lost decisively to Sheridan's 35,000–40,000-man Army of the Shenandoah at Third Winchester on September 19, at Fisher's Hill three days later, and at Cedar Creek on October 19. The last of these battles followed a period called "the burning," during which the Federals put much of the lower Valley to the torch. At Cedar Creek, Early planned and executed a complex offensive that routed two-thirds of the more numerous Federals before Sheridan orchestrated a stunning counterattack.

Cedar Creek ended major military operations in the Valley and provoked widespread complaints about Early's leadership. Old Jube remained detached from Lee's army, commanding a small force that suffered a final humiliating defeat at Waynesboro on March 2, 1865. Although Lee expressed continued confidence in Early's "ability, zeal, and devotion to the cause," he knew that the Confederate people did not. They blamed Early for the loss of the Valley, focusing on his failures and ignoring the odds against which he had contended. A woman who saw Early shortly after Waynesboro confided to her diary: "Oh! How are the mighty fallen! Gen. Early came in town this evening with six men having been hid somewhere in the mountains. He used to be a very great man." Removed from command and directed in late March 1865 to return to Rocky Mount and await further orders, Early missed the surrender of Lee's army at Appomattox.[14]

Early felt the sting of late-war popular disapprobation keenly, and criticism from Virginians almost certainly cut deepest because state loyalty had been a polestar for much of his life. He took pride in the Commonwealth and his family's associations with it. "[O]ur ancestors won this country from savage life," he wrote shortly after the war, "and started Virginia on that career which rendered her so prosperous, happy, and renowned." In 1850, while opposing transfer of a measure of power from slaveholders to non-slaveholders in the state government, he asserted that Virginia had been good to his family and other residents, affording "ample protection for our persons and our property"—a good thing, because "were it not for the existence of property and its due protection, society could not remain in an organized state, for any considerable length of time." Apart from his time at West Point and short stints in the army, in Mexico, and in Mississippi pursuing a legal case, he had lived in Virginia and taken an active, if usually unsuccessful, role in politics. His figure, stooped because of painful arthritis while still in his forties, was a familiar one in his part of the state, and he earned widespread respect as one who had discharged military responsibilities during the war with Mexico. His election as a delegate to the state convention in 1861 occasioned favorable notice from the most important newspaper in the area. "Eleven hundred majority for the conservative ticket!" reported Lynchburg's *Virginian:* "Who would have thought it?" The editor congratulated "our valued friend, the Major, on his victory. We expect to see him looking ten years younger and walking, brisk and erect, without his cane."[15]

The convention afforded Early a platform from which to assert his loyalty to Virginia. A witness who saw him board a train at Big Lick (modern Roanoke) for the trip to Richmond noted, "Major Early was so hoarse from excessive canvassing against secession that he could hardly speak above a whisper." Secession represented to him an unjustifiable break with the Constitution that might affect the stability of Virginia's society, and he repeatedly extolled the virtues of the existing system. Sometimes he stressed economics at the convention, as when he predicted that the loss of northern markets would hurt Virginia's tobacco industry (a key segment of the economy in his part of the state). He also raised the specter of uncertain control over slaves held in far western and northwestern Virginia, where the free soil of Ohio and Pennsylvania might beckon those seeking to escape bondage. That line of argument contained a self-interested dimension because Joab Early had moved to the Kanawha Valley. "I have an aged father living within thirteen miles of the Ohio," commented Early in late April, "with some thirty or forty negroes, and in the most exposed portion of that region."[16]

When state rights advocates among the delegates raised their banner in support of secession, Early turned the point against them by suggesting the Confederacy might take military actions to compromise the Commonwealth's territorial and governmental integrity. Were a Confederate army "to march through Virginia to sustain the rights of Virginia . . . ," stated Early with more than a hint of sarcasm, "I ask how is this proposition . . . to redress our wrongs and assert our rights, to coincide with any idea of State Rights?"

And when a delegate who claimed "to be of the State Rights school" threatened to join the Confederacy whatever the decision of the Virginia convention, Early rejoined: "What, sir, becomes of all these pretensions of devotion to Virginia? I acknowledge my fealty to Virginia. I intend to stand by her . . . whatever may be her destiny weal or woe."[17]

The stormy weeks of March and April tested Early's firm allegiances to what he considered two legitimate governments—those of Virginia and the United States. He gave his fullest expression of loyalty to Virginia on April 6. "I trust in God," he told the convention in language even stronger than Lee had chosen to explain his decision to resign from the U.S. Army, "that when Virginia's hour of trial does come, I will have the nerve and the ability to do my duty. My fortunes are with her, and shall ever be with her, under all circumstances. . . . I shall neither desert her in her hour of prosperity, her hour of adversity, her hour of glory, or her hour of shame. She is my mother, and I will stand by her under all circumstances." He expected Abraham Lincoln to make as firm a statement in favor of the nation. Should Virginia send a delegation demanding to know "what is to be his course of policy," as some in the convention recommended, Early thought the new president, if he possessed even "a particle of pride" or "a particle of manhood," would say he was responsible to the whole country and not "to the Convention of Virginia."[18]

To the end, Early maintained that true Virginians would resist secession. Members of the convention cast three pivotal votes. On April 4, a test ballot on secession failed by a 2–1 margin, with Early among those opposed. On April 17, five days after the firing on Fort Sumter and two after Lincoln's call for seventy-five thousand volunteers to put down the rebellion, the delegates voted 88–55 in favor of secession. Early was among the fifty-five nays. On April 25, the convention voted 76–19 to adopt the Confederate constitution, with Early part of the shrunken opposition. He had staked out his position on April 16, in anticipation of the next day's decisive ballot. "I have sat in my seat all day, and imagined that I could see a ball of flame hanging over this body," he told his fellow delegates, pronouncing secession "a great crime . . . against the cause of liberty and civilization." Support for the Union was "in the interest of my country, in the interest of my State, and in the interest of the cause of liberty itself." Departing from the Union, he warned, would bring "such a war as this country has never seen."[19]

Yet once the die was cast, only a single option remained in Early's mind. His votes on the convention's three crucial ballots had upheld Unionist principles; the state's majority decision and Lincoln's actions changed everything. Just as he had opposed war with Mexico and then volunteered to serve, so also did he acknowledge a duty to sustain Virginia in this new crisis. He would yield his patriotic submission to its authorities and thereby make good on his promise voiced in the convention on April 6. His military training and experience positioned him in the forefront of delegates who began addressing the state's defensive needs. On April 22, Early enthusiastically supported Governor Letcher's nomination of Robert E. Lee to head all state forces. "I have opposed the act of secession at every step," he needlessly reminded fellow delegates, ". . . yet as a Convention of my State has decided in favor of that act of secession, and as we are now engaged in this contest, all my wishes, all my desires and all the energies of my hand and heart will be given to the cause of my State." Whether or not Virginia had "the right of secession or revolution," Early noted, "I want to see my State triumphant. I do believe it will be triumphant under the lead of Major-General Lee." Eleven days later, Early informed Governor Letcher of his wish "to contribute as far as I can to the defense of the State if it shall be invaded." Commissioned a colonel of Virginia state forces, he began organizing volunteers in Lynchburg and soon took the field at the head of a brigade.[20]

Early signed the ordinance of secession in late May (after Virginia's voters had ratified it), taking the opportunity to explain his reasons. Lincoln's call for volunteers and other aggressive policies had "set aside the Constitution and laws and subverted the government of the United States," he claimed in language that recalled his 1835 letter concerning Santa Anna's treatment of Texas. The Republican president headed a usurped government founded "on the worst principles of tyranny," and Early affixed his signature to the ordinance "with the intention of sustaining the liberties, independence and entity of the State of Virginia." He continued to hope, however, for "a reconstruction of the old Union in any manner that shall unite the people of Virginia with the people of the non-slave states of the North." Five years later, Early recalled that adoption of the ordinance "wrung from me bitter tears of grief."[21]

Early's devotion to the nation was genuine, an outgrowth of his belief that the Constitution safeguarded the liberty of white citizens to have a voice in their own governance and to amass and enjoy property. Moreover, the founders had established a nation that protected the liberty of those in the political minority, which resonated powerfully with Early. When secessionists claimed that only departure from the Union would protect the white South's minority rights, he would have none of it. "I have been in a minority all my life," he remarked in reference to his membership in the Whig Party. "I have been standing up against currents that few men of my humble capacity could withstand, in defence of the rights of the minority." But secession represented the wrong method of preserving the rights of the southern minority. "[C]an these rights be asserted, not by force or violence, but under the Constitution and according to the laws?" he asked rhetorically. "I think they can."[22]

Like Robert E. Lee, Early deprecated extremists from North and South as potential menaces to the nation's well-being. During heated controversies relating to what became the Compromise of 1850, he initially endorsed President Zachary Taylor's efforts to quiet the shrill debate over whether California should be a free state and the New Mexico Territory organized on the basis of popular sovereignty. "I sincerely hope that the efforts of the disunionists in both Quarters of the country to produce trouble, may be unavailing," he observed in early January 1850, ". . . I think the great body of the people will be ready to stand by the President in his pledges to sustain the Union in its integrity." Shortly thereafter, when it seemed the slaveholding Taylor conceded too much to Free Soilers, Early backed away from him. Similarly, he later explained that "conservative men" rejected popular sovereignty as a solution to the Kansas-Nebraska turmoil of the mid-1850s because it could revive "the fires of the former agitation" regarding slavery in the territories. Throughout the 1840s and 1850s, he resolutely sought a middle course and was offended by abolitionists and, to a lesser degree, by southern fire-eaters and others who seemed unconcerned with national political stability. At odds with many of his class in the South, he did not consider California's admission as a free state—a central feature of the Compromise of 1850—a harbinger of ruin. He even contemplated moving there or to New Mexico Territory if the Fillmore administration would appoint him a district attorney.[23]

Unlike Dodson Ramseur and growing numbers of his southern contemporaries, Early opposed radical positions on issues related to slavery. He admired Millard Fillmore, a New Yorker, as a "patriot and statesman" who had pursued a "prudent, wise and national course" as president when dealing with intemperate proslavery and antislavery critics during the vituperative debates surrounding the Compromise of 1850. Early hoped all divisions related to the peculiar institution would give way before a common resolve to honor the Constitution. That document explicitly protected property in slaves and, excepting the foreign slave trade and the guarantee for the return of fugitive slaves, "left its regulation in every particular, where it belonged, that is to the several states where it existed." If northern states that had abolished slavery did not wish to be allied with those that retained it, they should have voted against ratification of the Constitution. "Having ratified it," concluded Early in a posthumously published essay, "the faith of those states became pledged to every consideration that can bind states as communities, or men as individuals, to respect the institutions, rights and property of the other states and to faithfully abide by all of the compromises and guarantees of the Constitution."[24]

Early seldom resorted to antinorthern cant during the antebellum years, applauding what he deemed properly conservative opinions and actions regardless of a person's geographical location. Thus could he support Fillmore while criticizing Virginia-born Zachary Taylor and an array of extreme state rights advocates from the Deep South. For anyone acquainted only with Early's wartime and postwar careers, when he habitually deployed anti-Yankee invective, his previous moderation might seem surprising.

He reached a crossroads in this respect following John Brown's raid on Harpers Ferry in October 1859. For Early, no antebellum event more starkly underscored the absence of respect for the Constitution than the northern response to Brown's failed operation. Early helped organize a public meeting in Rocky Mount on December 5, three days after Brown's execution in Charles Town, Virginia. Speaking to a large crowd comprising people from across the political spectrum, he explained why they had been summoned to meet. Brown's "wicked and diabolical" actions had threatened "to inaugurate a servile insurrection upon the soil of Virginia, for the purpose of destroying by force the institution of domestic slavery as it exists among us." Alarmingly, the raid "seems to have met with the sympathy and approbation of a large number of Northern people," averred Early, and not to "have been properly rebuked by any considerable portion of them."[25]

Although Brown's immediate target had been in Virginia, Early reminded listeners that the social structure of the entire South had come under attack. Slavery was a domestic institution and should not be subject to interference from the North in the form of "moral suasion, legislative enactment, or physical force." Yet many northern citizens chose to ignore the guarantees of the Constitution, leaving "the citizens of the South . . . [to] do all in their power to resist such interference." Early recommended that Virginia be "put in a complete state of defense" by having all able-bodied men arm themselves "with a good rifle or other fire arm." If necessary, citizens of the Commonwealth would "cheerfully submit to any amount of taxation that may be necessary to place the State in an efficient defensive position." A series of resolutions calculated to guard against future incursions carried unanimously.[26]

Brown's raid had threatened an institution Early believed fundamental to maintaining an ordered society in the South—and thus it brought to the fore his white southern identity. Early is a perfect example of those who owned few or no slaves but nonetheless strongly supported the institution. The federal manuscript census returns for 1840, 1850, and 1860 show no property in slaves for Early, while the 1846 personal property tax list for Franklin County includes among his holdings one slave over twelve years old. A relative observed after the war that Early "was never an investor in slaves, although he always possessed a negro servant." But he worried about the sanctity of property in general and about his family's extensive slaveholdings in particular. One of his objections to secession, as already noted, was concern about the security of property in slaves held by his father and other Virginians living near Ohio or Pennsylvania.[27]

Perhaps equally important, Early considered slavery the best means of controlling several million African Americans who lived in the antebellum South. In this opinion, he aligned exactly with Robert E. Lee and Dodson Ramseur. By the late eighteenth century, Early wrote shortly after the war, abolition would have menaced white society and the American economy. "[T]he slaves bore such a proportion to the white population and the whole business of the country was so identified with their labor," he commented, "that it was impossible to emancipate them, without entailing on both races evils far greater than those supposed to result from the existence of slavery itself." The founding generation recognized this, shielded slave property in the Constitution, and wisely chose not to embrace what Early called "the dangerous experiment of the ideal schemes of a false philanthropy." In making this determination, "many statesmen of the South and especially of Virginia" who "deplored slavery as an evil . . . that at some future time . . . might be abolished" reluctantly accepted their inability to "suggest any mode for doing so."[28]

Many white southerners muted their opinions about the "positive good" of slavery after the war, but Early never did so. Instead, while living in Canada during the early postwar period, he drafted an analysis that rooted the institution in the ancient world and argued that charges of its sinfulness were a relatively recent phenomenon. Although largely nonreligious himself, Early grounded key parts of his argument in the Bible. He traced the derivation of the word "slave" to prove that it should be equated with "servant" and quoted numerous Old and New Testament passages to bolster his conclusion that slavery and Christianity were entirely compatible. When Moses received the law of God through the Commandments, wrote Early, the Lord protected property in menservants and maidservants through the tenth commandment: "Thus did that same God who had shown favor to Abraham, and Lot, and Isaac, and Jacob, and Job, all slave-holders, without once rebuking them because they held their fellow man in bondage, give his express sanction to the institution of domestic slavery, by positive law." He did note that Christianity brought one significant change. In the pre-Christian era, masters had power over the slave's life as well as his person; Christianity revoked the former and thus ameliorated the institution in settings such as the antebellum South.[29]

Early closed his analysis with volleys against both the abolitionists who had attacked slavery and the white southerners—former Confederates—who had voiced doubts about religious justifications for slavery. "It was reserved for the philanthropists of the 19th century," he stated mockingly, "who endeavor to pervert the scriptures to suit their own theories, to make the wonderful discovery that the slavery of the African or negro race, a race that has never, without the agency of slavery, produced a single civilized being, is against the spirit of Christianity." As for "African slavery . . . in the states composing the late Confederate states," Early disparaged "some, even among the most faithful adherents of those states in the late struggle, who have become so faint-hearted as to acknowledge that slavery must have been wrong, or Providence would not have permitted us to be overwhelmed in disaster, and slavery itself to be exterminated." The outcome of the war, he countered, did not prove Providence punished the Confederacy "because of the wrong and injustice of African slavery." To the contrary, emancipation represented a "grievous wrong" because "Providence has no more condemned us on account of slavery, and therefore permitted our overthrow by our enemies, than it condemned Job, the 'perfect and upright man,' when he was permitted to be so sorely afflicted by Satan. In the dispensations of Providence, it has repeatedly happened that the right has failed, and wrong has been triumphant."[30]

Early joined most white southerners (and white northerners) in accepting the unquestioned superiority of his own race. The creator had marked black people "with a different colour and an inferior physical and mental organization." Any mixing of the races would contravene the Lord's design, he thought. A passage in the preface to his 1866 memoir encapsulates his thinking on the subject: "Reason, common sense, true humanity to the black, as well as the safety of the white race, required that the inferior race should be kept in a state of subordination."[31]

Although Early believed it vital to maintain a social structure predicated on slavery, his antebellum identity as a southerner surely fell short of Ramseur's—and perhaps of Lee's as well. He would become as unwavering a Confederate as the other two, but Virginia and the nation stood first and second with him until 1861, and there seems no reason to doubt his anguish at cutting ties with the United States. As a candidate for the Virginia convention, he had announced in Rocky Mount: "When I die, I wish to be buried in the flag of the United States which I bore in Florida and Mexico." Only his sense of honor and the "dignity of Virginia" persuaded him to abandon "the attachment of a lifetime to that Union which had been cemented by the blood of so many patriots, and which I had been accustomed to look upon (in the language of Washington) as the palladium of the political safety and prosperity of the country." For him, as for Lee, the defining loyalty in choosing secession was to his home state.[32] For both, the decisive vote in the Virginia convention on April 17 was crucial. Although he opposed secession even at that point, Early viewed the majority's decision as binding. State thus trumped nation, and his willingness to oppose the old flag followed naturally from his antebellum beliefs. Because Lincoln's actions beginning on April 15 violated Early's conception of the constitutional compact between the United States and Virginia—to which he always had turned for protection of property and civil order—he felt duty bound to stand by his state and accompany it into the Confederacy.

Several themes emerged during Early's four-year commitment to the Confederate war. Convinced by May 1861 that the Lincoln administration had left the Constitution in tatters, he saw the Confederacy as a conservative bulwark protecting the liberty and property of white southerners. His belief in a patriotic submission to legitimate authority created disdain for anyone who gave less than full allegiance to the new nation, and he heaped particular scorn on secessionists who evinced only tepid national sentiment. The old Unionist showed no more patience with white southerners who maintained their antebellum loyalty to the United States, lambasting them as Tories betraying their people. His attitude toward the northern government and people also hardened as the scale and violence of the conflict escalated, ripening into an unadulterated hatred by the time of Appomattox. This hardening was evident throughout the Confederacy, including with Lee and Ramseur, but assumed a more extreme form with Early.

Early thought Lincoln's actions in the spring and early summer of 1861 inaugurated "an odious despotism" that allowed, even demanded, resort to "the right of resistance and revolution as exercised by our fathers in 1776." He adopted "the cause of the whole Confederacy with equal ardour" to that which had prompted him to enter Virginia's military service "willingly, cheerfully, zealously." Unwavering in his Confederate loyalty, he proved unwilling "to consent to any compromise or settlement short of the absolute independence of my country."[33]

Early approved of stringent measures to maintain the war effort, with the central government taking the lead and states—including Virginia—doing whatever necessary to assist the larger national project. The issue of manpower illustrates his approach. In February 1862, with the expiration of one-year enlistments approaching, he called for greater action from both the Davis administration and Virginia's legislature. "Our army here is fast disappearing," he informed James L. Kemper, a colonel who also served as speaker of Virginia's House of Delegates, "and I do not see adequate measures adopted to recruit it." In addition, many officers "who ought to set an example to their men of devotion to duty from a sense of honour, and submission to privation . . . apparently regard only their personal convenience and comfort." Early thought this "a painful state of things to exist in an army that is fighting for its homes and the very existence of its country." As for the Virginia legislature, too many members thought of nothing but holding on to their seats when "the question really is whether there shall be any seats for them to fill."[34]

Later in the war, Early complained to Adjutant and Inspector General Samuel Cooper about men serving in the army who sought various state or local exemptions from national service. He used as examples from his own command a man from Rockingham County, Virginia, who had procured a job as the jailor in his community and another who had been elected a justice of the peace. This class of men who schemed to avoid conscription by obtaining positions exempted from the draft should be thwarted, insisted Early, who argued that no state had the authority to remove men from the national armies in this way.[35]

An anecdote about Early's rigid stance on conscription gained wide circulation. In January 1865, the general and members of his staff attended a church service in Staunton, Virginia. Toward the end of the sermon, the clergyman closed his Bible, raised his right hand, and emphatically asked the congregation: "Suppose, my Christian friends, that those who have laid for centuries in their graves should arise now and come forth from their quiet resting places; and marching in their white shrouds should pass before this congregation, by thousands and tens of thousands, what would be the result?" Early leaned over to a member of his staff and in a stage whisper answered, "Ah! I'd conscript every damned one of them."[36]

Early directed biting criticism toward secessionists who chose safety over military risk. In early 1862, he read newspaper articles "warmly urging the propriety of electing to the positions of ease and comfort in the government only such men as were original secessionists." He classified these individuals, "safely ensconced at home in comfort & ease," with other rear-echelon shirkers but thought them especially craven because of their dramatic posturing during the crisis of 1860–61. James L. Kemper tried to reassure Early that "there is no danger of the stay-at-home fire-eaters monopolizing the honour of the country. They are destined to *roost low* the balance of their days." Some of Early's pessimism seems to have rubbed off on Kemper, however, who confessed to being in "very low spirits" and worrying whether "we are to have a country." Kemper mustered some weak optimism but saw ahead "disasters and bloody trials and suffering such as few peoples are shown in the history of the world to have undergone."[37]

Prominent secessionists who became important Confederate military figures sometimes felt Early's barbs. During the retreat of his Army of the Valley after the battle of Third Winchester in September 1864, he targeted Maj. Gen. John C. Breckinridge, who had been James Buchanan's vice president and headed the southern Democrats' presidential ticket in 1860. Riding slowly through the night, surrounded by bedraggled and silent infantrymen, Early turned to his lieutenant and muttered: "General Breckinridge, what do you think of the 'rights of the South in the Territories' now?" Much earlier in the conflict, as Gen. Joseph E. Johnston's army retreated from Centreville past the estate of a man who had trumpeted the need to demand slavery's extension into all the territories, Early "saw his old antagonist looking disconsolately over his broad fields, soon to be ravaged and destroyed by the enemy." Hailing the man, Early deployed the same taunt: "Well . . . what do you think of *the rights in the territories* this morning?"[38]

Persistent Unionists received much rougher treatment from Early. They had aligned themselves with the enemy, and he pronounced them "traitors" who profaned the "humblest private soldier who fought in the ranks of the Confederate Army" and "the grateful women for whose homes he fought." Early's journey from Virginia to Texas at the end of the war took him through Unionist parts of Alabama. In a diary he kept during the trip, he noted on June 21, 1865: "Got dinner at Hiram Smith's a vile old Tory in Fayette, we passed for Yankees and he charged us no bill. . . . All of this part of Alabama is for Union." Three days later in Greensboro he saw "the U.S. flag (a caricature of it) made by some tories, was flying. This is notorious tory country." Maj. Gen. George H. Thomas, a native of Southampton County, Virginia, ranked second only to Lt. Gen. Winfield Scott among southern officers who retained their Union loyalty. When Thomas died in 1870, Early brushed aside attempts to find something positive in his life and career. "I think the names of all who fought against their own states in such a war as was made by us," he wrote about three months after Thomas's death, "deserve to be consigned to eternal infamy anyhow."[39]

Union military operations and political actions proved the greatest spurs to Early's deepening sense of Confederate loyalty. Every Federal transgression—as defined by him—against the sanctity of property and the stable social and racial order of the antebellum years strengthened his national identity and nourished his loathing of the North and northerners. During the Mexican War, Early had gained experience with an enemy's civilian population when he served for two months as military governor of Monterrey. He prided himself on the fact that he established excellent relations with the Mexicans under his control. "It was generally conceded by officers of the army and Mexicans," he asserted, "that better order reigned in the city during the time I commanded there, than had ever before existed, and the good conduct of my men won for them universal praise."[40]

Federal armies during the Civil War exhibited behavior that differed markedly from Early's model of fair treatment of an enemy's population and its property. He condemned the destructive activities of soldiers commanded by David Hunter and Philip H. Sheridan in the Shenandoah Valley during the summer and fall of 1864. In the track of Hunter's army in June, pursuing Confederates witnessed scenes "truly heart-rending. Houses had been burned, and helpless women and children left without shelter. The country had been stripped of provisions and many families left without a morsel to eat." Early labeled Hunter's depredations "wanton, cruel, unjustifiable, and cowardly" and refused to "insult the memory of the ancient barbarians . . . by calling them 'acts of Vandalism.'" Sheridan perpetrated more widespread destruction between Winchester and Harrisonburg in early October. He "commenced burning barns, mills and stacks of small grain and hay, and the whole country was smoking."[41]

Early ordered northern civilian property to be burned on two well-known occasions. During the Confederate march through Pennsylvania in June 1863, his soldiers destroyed an ironworks owned by Thaddeus Stevens, the prominent Radical Republican congressman. The following summer, cavalrymen attached to his command put Chambersburg, Pennsylvania, to the torch. Taking full responsibility for both actions, Early justified the first on the grounds that Federals "invariably burned such works in the South, wherever they had penetrated." As for Chambersburg, Early explained to the city's leaders that he was levying a penalty of one hundred thousand dollars in gold or five hundred thousand dollars in "current Northern funds" in recompense for destruction ordered by General Hunter. "In default of the payment of this money," he warned, "your town is directed to be laid in ashes in retaliation for the burning of . . . houses of citizens of Virginia by Federal authorities." Chambersburg did not come up with the money, and Brig. Gen. John McCausland, in charge of part of Early's cavalry, carried out the orders on July 30. "I now came to the conclusion that we had stood this mode of warfare long enough," Early wrote in his memoirs of the actions of Hunter and others, "and that it was time to open the eyes of the people of the North to its enormity, by an example in the way of retaliation."[42]

Forced emancipation figured prominently in Early's growing animus against Yankees. In Virginia and across the rest of the Confederacy, it swept away billions of dollars in property and raised the possibility of black challenges to white supremacy. Joab Early was among the first Confederate civilians to experience this aspect of the war. In August 1861, as Union forces marched through the Kanawha Valley, he became a refugee, leaving "all my property except Joe who I took with me to assist." The other slaves remained behind, far removed from Joab's reach unless Confederates reclaimed the valley. In January 1863, Joab wrote again to his son, from Lynchburg, to say he had heard all was quiet in the Kanawha Valley. Lincoln's recent proclamation had exempted the forty-eight counties of western Virginia that would soon become West Virginia, which gave the elder Early some hope that he would not lose all his slaves. "I suppose as Lincoln has not set the negroes free then there will be no great stir among them for a while," he speculated. "[A]s the people in Ohio won't let them pass into the interior of the state a good many had returned but say they came to get their clothes and not to stay."[43]

Although concerned with his father's plight, Early worried more about the social tremors that could accompany emancipation. No topic elicited more vitriolic outbursts than how the United States had achieved the eradication of slavery in the Confederacy. Early's letter to John C. Breckinridge in March 1867 reveals the depth of his anger. In it, he fulminated against "the infernal demons who sit at Washington in unrestrained power"—the class of leaders who had pushed for emancipation and brought social upheaval to the South. Jim Crow lay far in the future, and former Confederates were uncertain about their ability to maintain racial control. "A very small portion of the civilized world is guiltless in regard to the wrongs done our people," fumed Early from Toronto, "and I want to see all the nations punished for their folly & wicked inter-meddling in regard to the institution of slavery, about the propriety, advantages and justice of which my opinion daily grows stronger." He longed for "a great convulsion of some sort. If I could see society upturned from its very foundations all over the world, I would rejoice at it." Wartime hostility toward northerners had reached a toxic intensity for Early, who claimed he "would like to begin the fight over right now, though with the certainty that we would be exterminated. I have got to that condition, that I think I could scalp a Yankee woman and child without winking my eyes."[44]

Early blamed radical northern propagandists for poisoning Europeans on the subject of slavery. If only the Confederacy had instituted abolition on its own, some foreigners argued, diplomatic recognition and perhaps independence would have followed. For Early and other white southerners who always had depended on slavery to control millions of black people, such a proposition brought to mind images of domestic chaos. The value of diplomatic recognition paled in comparison to the economic and social benefits the Confederacy derived from slavery. Turning to a literary example to clinch his point, Early offered the experience of Don Quixote, who freed the galley slaves but then had to defend himself against them. "What could the people of the South have done in the prosecution of the war," asked Early, "if 3,000,000 slaves had been turned loose among them and the whole labor system of the country deranged?" With the defeat of the Confederacy and "slavery violently abolished" by northern fanatics, wrote Early as he surveyed the immediate postwar landscape, "inconceivable miseries have been entailed on the white race." Future chroniclers of history would be left "to wonder at the follies and crimes committed in this generation."[45]

Early emerged from the war an ardent Confederate nationalist without a country. Unwilling "to live under the same government with the Yankees," as he put it in October 1865, he also feared he might be prosecuted because of the burning of Chambersburg. So he spent four years abroad, settling in 1866 near Toronto, Canada, where he mused and wrote about his part in the turbulent period from secession through Appomattox. Poor and lonely much of the time, he lamented the possibility that a black political class might rise in the former Confederacy and sometimes slipped into very dark moods. Letters to his brother Sam chronicled Early's pessimism. At the beginning of 1868, he worried that elections in Alabama could settle the fate of the rest of the South. If "Alabama becomes Africanized," he predicted, there would be no hope. A few months earlier, in one of his grimmest moments, he wrote about Confederate soldiers who had died in uniform and thus been spared seeing the end of their nation: "Really, I have long felt that those who fell like poor Rodes, Ramseur & others during the war, were more fortunate than the balance of us who survived."[46]

Unlike Robert E. Lee, Early never counseled others to accept the verdict of the battlefield, support the forced national reunion in good faith, and look to a future unencumbered with pointless might-have-beens. He tempered his comments to Lee, but anger nonetheless seeped into his letters. "Permit me to express my gratification at the dignified course you have observed since the cessation of active hostilities," he wrote his old chief in late 1868. "It is one that has commanded admiration in all quarters." Yet other parts of the letter indicated how far apart the two men stood. "The enemy (for such the mass of northern people are to us) is persecuting our people," declared Early, "with even more vindictive hatred than during the war, when we had arms in our hands." Turning to the subject of wrenching social and political changes since the war, he added, "It would have been far more magnanimous and humane to have hung or beheaded every one of our leaders, both Civil and Military, and then given peace to the mass of the people, than to have attempted to degrade and humiliate them. . . . Death is not by any means the worst fate that can befall a man, or a people."[47]

Early returned to the United States in 1869 and soon settled in Lynchburg, where he remained until his death in 1894. During the last decades of his life, he frequently referred to the Confederacy as his "country" and regretted the loss of the old slaveholding society's unchallenged white supremacy. As late as 1885 he lashed out at Thomas L. Rosser, a cavalry general who had served under him in the Valley in 1864, for speaking about "the stain of slavery." The comment left Early "surprised that I ever entertained the idea that he had any of the attributes of manhood." A few years later, Maj. Gen. George Crook met Early in Lynchburg and recorded some thoughts in his diary. The two had opposed one another in the Shenandoah Valley, and Crook subsequently earned considerable fame in campaigns against Native Americans. "We met Gen. Jubal Early, the ex-Confederate Gen.," noted Crook, who described the seventy-three-year-old as "much stooped and enfeebled, but as bitter and virulent as an adder. He has no use for the government or for the northern people. Boasts of his being unreconstructed, and that he won't accept a pardon for his rebellious offenses."[48]

A lucrative connection with the Louisiana Lottery from the mid-1870s until his death afforded Early a comfortable living, freeing him to write and lecture extensively. As president of the Southern Historical Society and of the Association of the Army of Northern Virginia, frequent speaker, and indefatigable controversialist, he did as much as any other individual to shape the Lost Cause interpretation of the war. He celebrated Robert E. Lee's military accomplishments, attributed the constitutional high ground to the Confederacy, praised the Whiggish slaveholding civilization of Virginia and the Old South, and dismissed U. S. Grant and other Union generals as minimally gifted soldiers who won only because of their massive advantages of men and material resources. He never apologized for any of his decisions or actions. Dressed in gray suits with cufflinks featuring enameled St. Andrew's Cross battle flags and thoroughly immersed in the history of the war, he became, for many, the personification of the Confederacy. Shortly after his return from Canada, a newspaper editor enthused, "General Early commands our admiration for his undying pluck. He is Confederate and Virginian to the back-bone. He hung out after nearly everybody else had succumbed."[49]

Jubal Early offers a perfect example of someone from the tumultuous years of the mid-nineteenth century whose loyalties changed although his opinions about political and social questions remained largely static. He never deviated from his beliefs in the Constitution as it had been, the correctness of slavery, rule by a propertied elite, and the need for white supremacy in a biracial society. His loyalties should be read with this consistency in mind. He embraced the Union until Lincoln's actions in the spring of 1861, the antebellum South unless its leaders acted in what he considered radical ways that threatened stability, the Confederacy as a shield against the Republican threat, and always Virginia, which I believe proved more central to Early's equation of loyalties than it did to Lee's or than North Carolina did to Ramseur's. "[A] man who did nothing by halves," as a close subordinate observed, ". . . his decision once made was as to him, a decree of faith." His successive and overlapping loyalties, all firmly and honestly held, remind us of the complexity of mid-nineteenth-century American identities and how they shaped reactions to great events.[50]

CHAPTER FOUR

For His Country and His Duty

Confederate National Sentiment beyond Appomattox

Robert E. Lee and Jubal A. Early occupied critical positions in the story of how Confederate national sentiment persisted in the postwar decades. Stephen Dodson Ramseur, mortally wounded almost six months before Appomattox, was relegated to a secondary though still noteworthy place in the narrative. All had been committed nationalists, demanding collective sacrifice to establish a republic that promised long-term social and economic stability within a slave-based structure. Although scrupulous in his public call for acceptance of reunion, Lee became the centerpiece of a Lost Cause interpretation of the mid-nineteenth century that glorified the Confederacy and its white populace. Early did as much as any other individual—perhaps more—to refine and spread the message that Confederates had struggled admirably against fearsome odds, always with Lee and his army in the forefront of their national effort. Ramseur's impeccable credentials as a brave young commander and martyr resonated most strongly in North Carolina but also in other parts of the South.

How the three men, as actors and symbols, stoked feelings of postwar Confederate community brings us back to David Potter's observation about reluctance to ascribe genuine national sentiment to people or causes historians find distasteful. Undeniable evidence demonstrates that loyalty to the Confederacy, so widely apparent during the war, did not disappear with the surrenders of April and

May 1865. Brief consideration of that salient fact is necessary before turning to some final thoughts about Lee, Ramseur, and Early.

The people who had struggled for southern independence entered the postwar era as losers on an epic scale, yet many remained devoted to their failed cause. Well more than 250,000 of their men died in uniform,[1] emancipation seemingly ended their control over black people, and no one knew what political and economic penalties the triumphant North might impose. At a distance of almost 150 years, it is extremely difficult to recapture the degree to which Confederates imagined themselves in a world turned ominously upside down. Amid enormous uncertainty and with the Confederacy's formal institutions dismantled, the defeated population found ways to maintain public and private ties to their short-lived republic while reentering the United States during the era of Reconstruction.

Two accommodations to postwar reality stood paramount for ex-Confederates. The Union would be restored—that always had been the sine qua non of victory for the loyal citizenry of the United States—and slavery's end was assured. The mass of white northerners never embraced emancipation as a stand-alone moral goal during the conflict, but they had come to regard it as a necessary tool to defeat the Confederacy, punish the slaveholding class that had pushed for secession, and, within a postbellum context, protect the restored Union from future internal threat. Ratification of the Thirteenth Amendment in December 1865 settled the issue of black freedom definitively. Some historians have suggested the nation was restored with relative ease, thus underscoring the absence of meaningful national sentiment among Confederates. Reunion and reconciliation, goes a common argument, predominated by the late nineteenth century. In fact, the vanquished Rebels understood, far better than many modern scholars, that they had been so decisively defeated on the battlefield that their sole option was to accept reunion and the end of slavery.[2]

Like Robert E. Lee, they moved forward with reunion but seldom reached out in the spirit of true reconciliation. There is an important distinction to make here. "Reunion" and "reconciliation" never should be deployed as synonyms—the former entailed the political restoration of the wayward states, the latter a far more complicated phenomenon requiring emotional adjustments and letting go of the past. Most former Confederates never conceded that secession had been unconstitutional, and they mirrored both Lee and Early in harboring a firm belief, whether expressed publicly or not, that slavery had been the best method of dealing with a large black population and should not have been ended by forced emancipation.

Far from being easy, reunion played out as a tortuous process that lasted far longer then the actual war. It was marked by widespread violence and a determined effort by ex-Confederates, on the political and social fronts, to establish unequivocal white supremacy. Unable to reinstitute slavery, they settled for a watered-down version of what it had provided—a social structure within which white people exerted economic, legal, and social control over millions of black people. The Jim Crow South, a reality by the late nineteenth century, lasted for many decades and should be viewed as the most obvious expression of the Confederate generation's response to defeat and emancipation.[3]

While the effort to reassert racial control proceeded, former Confederates created organizations and traditions that evoked and celebrated their four-year struggle for independence. Much of the attention centered on common soldiers and famous generals. Scores of thousands of military dead were reinterred in sections of cemeteries that served as the southern equivalent of the national cemeteries constructed for the Union dead. Confederate Memorial Day (or Decoration Day), established within a year of the conflict's termination, offered an annual opportunity for elaborate programs of remembrance. The United Confederate Veterans and other groups brought together men who had shouldered muskets during the war. Annual "encampments" of veterans became important public events involving parades, speeches, and other activities. Monuments to soldiers and individual military units sprouted on innumerable courthouse grounds, typically bearing inscriptions inviting viewers to remember the Confederate war as an example of heroic striving against the odds. In the 1890s, Mississippi added the St. Andrew's Cross battle standard of the Army of Northern Virginia to its state flag, and Alabama and Florida changed their state flags to incorporate a red St. Andrew's Cross. Iconography also played a leading role in preserving ties to the conflict. A print titled *The Last Meeting of Lee and Jackson*, issued in 1879 and based on a painting by Everett B. D. Julio, featured the two Confederate paladins at Chancellorsville and achieved a ubiquitous presence in southern homes, as did other depictions of "Marse Robert" and his lieutenants.[4]

Lee the wartime nationalist dwarfed all other Rebels as a link to the Confederate saga. His death in October 1870 occasioned a flood of panegyrics. Three examples convey typical themes. In Georgia, former general Ambrose R. Wright told an audience they had lost "the truest and the most sublime hero whom the ages have produced." The Confederate nation had meant everything to Lee, continued Wright, and "it was the loss of his cause which finally sundered the heart-strings of the hero and drew him from earth to Heaven." At a rally in the St. Charles Theatre in New Orleans, the city's largest venue, a speaker rejoiced "that the South will hold his ashes. But his fame belongs to the human race. Washington, too, was born in the South and sleeps in the South. . . . We place the name of Lee by that of Washington." In Richmond, Jefferson Davis specifically countered the idea that Lee's loyalty was above all else to Virginia (while also inflating the number of Confederate states by four): "[T]hey do injustice to Lee who believe he fought only for Virginia. He was ready to go anywhere, on any service, for the good of his country; and his heart was as broad as the fifteen States struggling for the principles that our forefathers fought for in the Revolution of 1776."[5]

Although Lee had opposed erecting monuments, imposing ones dedicated to him went up in New Orleans in 1884 and in Richmond six years later. The unveiling in Richmond attracted at least one hundred thousand people, who watched a parade of between fifteen and twenty thousand participants that extended four miles and featured Confederate veterans and schoolchildren as well as notable guests. One of the general's admirers, writing years later and unafraid of a hyperbolic flourish, pronounced the celebration "an event in the world's history." A recumbent statue by Edward V. Valentine, commissioned by the Lee Memorial Association, drew dignitaries from across the former Confederacy for the unveiling at Washington and Lee University in 1883. Installed in a mausoleum on campus dedicated to Lee, Valentine's presentation of the hero asleep in the field became a favorite for tourists seeking to honor the Confederate past.[6]

The festivities accompanying the unveiling of Lee's statue in Richmond boasted many pictures of Washington and Lee, which attested to Virginians' handling of their homegrown hero. Just as former Confederates trumpeted Lee's national identity, so also did Virginians celebrate his well-known loyalty to the Commonwealth. He displaced Thomas Jefferson and Patrick Henry and all other famous Virginians in the state pantheon, taking his position next to Washington. Indeed, in the minds of most of the Civil War generation, Lee surpassed Washington. His birthday became a state holiday in 1889 (some other former Confederate states followed suit), and Lee later joined Washington as one of Virginia's two selections for inclusion in Statuary Hall in the U.S. Capitol. The author of a series of articles on "Virginians on Olympus" accurately captured the degree to which white Virginians elevated Lee. "Every schoolboy," wrote Marshall W. Fishwick in 1950, "knows the pronouncement of Light Horse Harry Lee about George Washington: 'First in war, first in peace, first in the hearts of his countrymen.' For many Southerners, and most Virginians, the tribute no longer belongs to a Washington who made the most of victory, but to the son of Light Horse Harry Lee, who made the most of defeat."[7]

Ironically, Lee also became an American hero, ending up alongside Abraham Lincoln as one of the conflict's two most popular figures. He did so despite neither regaining U.S. citizenship nor, it is safe to conjecture, rekindling his antebellum devotion to the nation of his father and Washington. His public acceptance of the battlefield's verdict made this possible, forging the image of a good loser among Americans who knew nothing of his private anger and frustration. Appomattox, where he and Grant deported themselves with equal grace, became widely understood as the moment when national healing began. The U.S. government soft-pedaled the unpleasant reality that Lee's cherished goal of Confederate nationhood would have permanently divided the nation. The Post Office put Lee on five stamps between the 1930s and the 1990s, and Congress designated Arlington House a shrine to his memory in the mid-1920s. The National Park Service handbook for the site, published in 1950 and revised twelve years later, described the Greek Revival structure as "a most appropriate national memorial to one of America's greatest men, Robert E. Lee." A booklet published in 1926 by the John Hancock Life Insurance Company of Boston struck a similar note in crafting an appeal to potential customers on both sides of the Potomac: "Today he is not merely a hero of the South; but to an undivided country he stands a great, an honored, and a beloved American."[8]

A small measure of irony also figured into the memory and commemoration of Dodson Ramseur. His primary allegiance unquestionably had been national during the war, with North Carolina occupying a distant second place. After Appomattox, however, he most often appeared as preeminently a North Carolinian. The Old North State led the way in commemorating his Confederate service. Because relatively few North Carolinians had achieved renown as generals, especially when compared to the number from Virginia, Ramseur stood out. The town of Columbia, located approximately thirty miles south of Greensboro, changed its name to Ramseur in the 1880s. In 1916, Mary Dodson Ramseur presented a portrait of her father to the state. Chief Justice Walter Clark of the North Carolina Supreme Court accepted the gift, alluding to Ramseur's Confederate loyalty: "I now present [this portrait] to the State to be hung on these walls in perpetual memorial that the generations to come may remember what manner of man he was who knew how to die for his country and his duty." Four years later, the North Carolina Historical Commission placed an impressive monument to Ramseur on the Valley Pike near Belle Grove. In the shadow of Massanutten Mountain on an autumn day, speakers cast Ramseur most obviously as a loyal North Carolinian. One predicted that "[a]s long as hearts throb, his sweet memory will live and breathe among the people of his native North Carolina." Former Union officer Henry A. du Pont also addressed the crowd, recalling days at West Point and Ramseur's last painful hours before closing with this: "Such, my friends, is the brief statement of my personal relations with that gallant soldier and splendid son of the old North State."[9]

Ramseur's widow and daughter afforded him visibility within North Carolina and beyond, buttressing his ties to state and failed nation. Ellen Richmond Ramseur donned the clothing of deep mourning in October 1864 and wore it until her death in 1900. In that respect, she functioned as a daily reminder in North Carolina of her husband's sacrifice. Mary Dodson Ramseur, who never married, traveled widely and participated in Lost Cause commemorations. A friend described her as "the idol . . . of the Confederate Veterans of the South," a woman of "unwavering devotion to the sacred cause of the Southern Confederacy." In 1922, she was chosen "Sponsor for the South" by the United Confederate Veterans for their Grand Reunion in Richmond—the "highest honor that can be bestowed by them, and the one most coveted and prized by the women of the South." *Confederate Veteran* magazine, which printed a portrait of Mary Ramseur on its cover, thought no more "gratifying appointment could have been made than of this daughter of the gallant Ramseur and fair daughter of the South." Connection with thousands of veterans who had fought for the national cause so important to her father permitted Mary Ramseur, in Richmond and elsewhere, to promote awareness of his principal loyalty.[10]

Few in the postwar years doubted Jubal Early's first loyalty. Self-consciously unreconstructed, he worked assiduously to shape future interpretations of the Confederacy. Long before historians discovered "memory" as an analytical lens, Early reminded ex-Confederates that what they said and wrote would influence future generations. He knew there would be a battle for the memory of the conflict, and he sought to position the Confederate nation favorably before the bar of history. Early clashed with sincere reconciliationists such as James Longstreet and John S. Mosby and also with situational reconciliationists—those who courted better sectional relations in public settings while holding private grudges—such as Fitzhugh Lee and John B. Gordon. He soon earned a reputation as a peerless defender of the Confederacy whose strident critiques of Union writings about the war pleased white southerners and outraged many in the North.

Few men admired Lee more than Early himself, who overlooked his old chief's public advice to move forward without rancor. He perfectly grasped that Lee represented the best card ex-Confederates could play. "[I]t is a vain work for us to seek anywhere for a parallel to the great character which has won our admiration and love," he stated in a famous 1872 address on the anniversary of Lee's birth: "Our beloved Chief stands, like some lofty column which rears its head among the highest, in grandeur, simple, pure and sublime, needing no borrowed lustre; and he is all our own." Despite defeat, white southerners could celebrate their efforts to build a new nation. "When asked for our vindication," affirmed Early, "we can triumphantly point to the graves of Lee and Jackson and look the world square in the face." He closed by charging his audience with a "sacred trust" of "cherishing the memory of our leaders and our fallen comrades."[11]

While Early endured a lonely exile in Canada in 1867, John Esten Cooke penned an apt tribute to his Confederate loyalty. A novelist and former member of Jeb Stuart's staff, Cooke insisted that "the brave and hardy Early" was due justice for his service to the southern nation. Throughout the conflict, Early remained "devoted to his country, and true as steel to the flag under which he fought—true to it in disaster and defeat as in success and victory." Cooke's sentiment enjoyed wide currency among ex-Confederates by the time of Early's death in 1894. The old warrior had become the quintessential Confederate, "a forceful and truthful writer of history," as a resolution from one camp of United Confederate Veterans put it. Flags in Richmond flew at half-staff to mark Early's passing, and cadets from the Virginia Military Institute fired a salute at his funeral in Lynchburg's Spring Hill Cemetery—proper gestures for a man whose state identity never had weakened. But Cooke, himself a Virginian, had it right. Jubal Early the Confederate, not the Virginian, held sway during the years when he left his greatest mark.[12]

The paths toward Confederate loyalty for Lee and Ramseur and Early help delineate important contours of American history from the late antebellum years through the end of the century. They highlight how Americans juggled multiple, often conflicting, loyalties. They reveal a white southern identity preoccupied with racial control that transcended political and class lines. They render it exceedingly difficult to argue the Confederacy should not be deemed a nation. Perhaps most important, they help us understand why and how Confederates waged a prodigiously bloody war and the manner in which they dealt with defeat.

Notes

꘤

Introduction

1. My biography of Ramseur was published by the University of North Carolina Press in 1985 as *Stephen Dodson Ramseur: Lee's Gallant General.*

2. One of the more influential studies arguing for the absence of Confederate nationalism was Richard E. Beringer, Herman Hattaway, Archer Jones, and William N. Still Jr., *Why the South Lost the Civil War* (Athens: University of Georgia Press, 1986). Emory M. Thomas, *The Confederate Nation, 1861–1865* (New York: Harper & Row, 1979), made the opposite case.

3. For a review of the literature relating to Confederate national sentiment, see Gary W. Gallagher, "Disaffection, Persistence, and Nation: Some Directions in Recent Scholarship on the Confederacy," *Civil War History* 55 (September 2009): 329–53.

4. Robert Grier Stephens Jr., ed., *Intrepid Warrior: Clement Anselm Evans, Confederate General from Georgia; Life, Letters, and Diaries of the War Years* (Dayton, Ohio: Morningside, 1992), 342–43; Eliza Frances Andrews, *The War-Time Journal of a Georgia Girl, 1864–1865* (1908; reprint, Lincoln: University of Nebraska Press, 1997), 371.

5. Edward L. Ayers's *Loyalty and America's Civil War* (Gettysburg, Pa.: Gettysburg College, Forty-Ninth Annual Robert Fortenbaugh Memorial Lecture, 2010) is a thoughtful meditation on the topic. For a perceptive look at one common soldier's relationship with the Confederate cause, see William L. Barney, *The Making of a Confederate: Walter Lenoir's Civil War* (New York: Oxford University Press, 2008).

6. David M. Potter, "The Historian's Use of Nationalism and Vice Versa," in Potter, *The South and the Sectional Conflict* (Baton Rouge: Louisiana State University Press, 1968), 34–86, quotations on pp. 56, 54, and 49. Potter gives the publishing history of his essay, which appeared in three versions, on p. vii.

7. Early made little attempt to hide the existence of the four children, whom he supported economically. For a brief discussion of this aspect of his life, see Charles C. Osborne, *Jubal: The Life and Times of General Jubal A. Early, CSA, Defender of the Lost Cause* (Chapel Hill, N.C.: Algonquin Books of Chapel Hill, 1992), 31–32.

8. The best starting place regarding the concept of honor remains Bertram Wyatt-Brown, *Southern Honor: Ethics and Behavior in the Old South* (New York: Oxford University Press, 1982). On Confederates and religion, a superb

overview is George C. Rable, *God's Almost Chosen Peoples: A Religious History of the American Civil War* (Chapel Hill: University of North Carolina Press, 2010).

9. On the importance of generation in the Civil War–era South, see Peter S. Carmichael, *The Last Generation: Young Virginians in Peace, War, and Reunion* (Chapel Hill: University of North Carolina Press, 2005). Carmichael's *Lee's Young Artillerist: William R. J. Pegram* (Charlottesville: University Press of Virginia, 1995) examines a Virginian whose attitudes closely resembled those of Ramseur.

10. The degree of postwar reconciliation between white people North and South has been much exaggerated. On this subject, see Caroline E. Janney, *Remembering the Civil War: Reunion and the Limits of Reconciliation* (Chapel Hill: University of North Carolina Press, 2013).

11. E. Merton Coulter, ed., *The Course of the South to Secession: An Interpretation by Ulrich Bonnell Phillips* (New York: D. Appleton-Century, 1939), 152. The quotation is from Phillips's essay titled "The Central Theme of Southern History," first presented as a paper at a meeting of the American Historical Association in 1928.

Chapter 1. Conduct Must Conform to the New Order of Things

1. Lee to P. G. T. Beauregard, October 3, 1865, in J. William Jones, *Life and Letters of Robert Edward Lee: Soldier and Man* (New York and Washington: Neale, 1906), 390. Although he must have doubted that history would treat his shifting loyalties as kindly as it had Washington's, Lee added, "He has not been branded by the world with reproach for this; but his course has been applauded."

2. Charles Francis Adams, *Three Phi Beta Kappa Addresses* (Boston: Houghton Mifflin, 1907), 81, 96–97; Charles Francis Adams, *Lee's Centennial: An Address by Charles Francis Adams Delivered at Lexington, Virginia Saturday, January 19, 1907, on the Invitation of the President and Faculty of Washington and Lee University* (Chicago: Arlington House, 1948), 24.

3. Douglas Southall Freeman, *R. E. Lee: A Biography*, 4 vols. (New York: Scribner's, 1934–35), 1:471, 441–42 (letter to Scott).

4. Terry L. Jones, *The American Civil War* (New York: McGraw-Hill Higher Education, 2010), 148; David Goldfield, *America Aflame: How the Civil War Created a Nation* (New York: Bloomsbury Press, 2011), 250; James M. McPherson, *Battle Cry of Freedom: The Civil War Era* (New York: Oxford University Press, 1988), 281; Thomas L. Connelly, *The Marble Man: Robert E. Lee and His Image in American Society* (New York: Knopf, 1977), 202.

5. Gary W. Gallagher, *Causes Won, Lost, and Forgotten: How Hollywood and Popular Art Shape What We Know about the Civil War* (Chapel Hill: University of North Carolina Press, 2008), 57–59, 72–73.

6. Freeman, *R. E. Lee*, 1:424–30.

7. Ibid., 431–34.

8. William Allan, "Memoranda of Conversations with General Robert E. Lee," in Gary W. Gallagher, ed., *Lee the Soldier* (Lincoln: University of Nebraska Press, 1995), 10; Freeman, *R. E. Lee*, 1:436–37. A former staff officer under Stonewall Jackson and member of the faculty at Washington College in Lexington, Allan spoke with Lee on February 25, 1868, immediately after which he made extensive notes of the session.

9. Freeman, *R. E. Lee*, 1:439–42; Allan, "Memoranda of Conversations," 10; Robert E. Lee, *The Wartime Papers of R. E. Lee*, ed. Clifford Dowdey and Louis H. Manarin (Boston: Little, Brown, 1961), 8–9.

10. Freeman, *R. E. Lee*, 1:442n39, 462–64.

11. Lee, *Wartime Papers*, 11; George H. Reese, ed., *Proceedings of the Virginia State Convention of 1861*, 4 vols. (Richmond: Virginia State Library, 1965), 4:369–70; Freeman, R. E. Lee, 1:464–66.

12. Reese, ed., *Proceedings*, 4:370–72. Lee, *Wartime Papers*, 11, includes a version of Lee's acceptance that differs in several ways from that in *Proceedings*.

13. Lee to Mrs. Anne Marshall, April 20, 1861, in Lee, *Wartime Papers*, 9–10; Elizabeth Brown Pryor, *Reading the Man: A Portrait of Robert E. Lee through His Private Letters* (New York: Viking, 2007), 291–93; Wayne Wei-Siang Hsieh, "'I Owe Virginia Little, My Country Much': Robert E. Lee, the United States Regular Army, and Unconditional Unionism," in Edward L. Ayers, Gary W. Gallagher, and Andrew J. Torget, eds., *Crucible of the Civil War: Virginia from Secession to Commemoration* (Charlottesville: University of Virginia Press, 2006), 35–37, 47.

14. Charles Royster, *Light-Horse Harry Lee and the Legacy of the American Revolution* (New York: Oxford University Press, 1981), 144–47; Henry Lee, *The Revolutionary War Memoirs of General Henry Lee* (1812; reprint, New York: Da Capo, 1998), 44–46. Da Capo reprinted the 1869 edition of the memoirs, which included a long biographical sketch of Henry Lee by Robert E. Lee and his brother Charles Carter Lee. For a concise treatment of Washington as a nationalist, see Joseph J. Ellis, *His Excellency George Washington* (New York: Knopf, 2004).

15. Lee to C. C. Lee, February 13, March 18, 1848, item 990B, box 1, Papers of Robert E. Lee, Albert and Shirley Small Special Collections Library, University of Virginia, Charlottesville (repository hereafter cited as Small Library, UVA).

16. Lee to Mrs. Lee, November 19, December 13, August 4, 1856, in Francis Raymond Adams Jr., ed., "An Annotated Edition of the Personal Letters of Robert E. Lee April, 1855–April, 1861" (PhD dissertation, University of Maryland, 1955; University Microfilms edition in 2 volumes), 1:201, 233, 142.

17. Lee to Winfield Scott, April 20, 1861, on the National Park Service website for Arlington House, Robert E. Lee Memorial, http://www.nps.gov/museum/exhibits/arho/exb/Military/ARHO-5623-Copy-of-RE-Lee-Le.html (accessed May 24, 2012); Lee to My dear Son, January 29, 1861, in William M. E. Rachal, ed., "'Secession is Nothing But Revolution': A Letter of R. E. Lee to His Son 'Rooney,'" *Virginia Magazine of History and Biography* 69 (January

1961): 6; Lee to Custis Lee [?], January 23, 1861, in J. William Jones, *Life and Letters of Robert Edward Lee*, 124.

18. Lee to Rooney Lee, January 29, 1861, in Rachal, ed., "Secession is Nothing But Revolution," 5; Allan, "Memoranda of Conversations," 9–11.

19. Lee to Mrs. Lee, December 27, 1856, in Adams Jr., ed., "Letters of Robert E. Lee," 1:244–46.

20. Ibid. On the literature that portrays Lee as opposed to slavery, see Alan T. Nolan, *Lee Considered: General Robert E. Lee and Civil War History* (Chapel Hill: University of North Carolina Press, 1991), chap. 2.

21. Lee to Samuel Cooper, December 24, 1859, in Adams Jr., ed., "Letters of Robert E. Lee," 2:556–57.

22. Gary W. Gallagher, ed., " 'We Are Our Own Trumpeters': Robert E. Lee Describes Winfield Scott's Campaign to Mexico City," *Virginia Magazine of History and Biography* 95 (July 1987): 772–73. On Lee and Talcott, see Freeman, *R. E. Lee*, 1:103–7, 122–27.

23. Lee, *Wartime Papers*, 388–90. Some historians have argued that Lee's comments to Seddon were inspired by Brig. Gen. Robert H. Milroy's inflammatory orders relating to suspected guerrillas in western Virginia. Although Lee was well aware of Milroy's pronouncements, I believe the language in his letter of January 10 indicates concern over much broader Federal policy. The verb "proclaimed" and reference to the possible "destruction" of the Confederacy's "social system" point—convincingly, in my opinion—toward the Emancipation Proclamation. However loathsome from Lee's point of view, Milroy scarcely strutted on a large enough stage to warrant such verbiage. For a discussion of the letter as a response to Milroy, see Nolan, *Lee Considered*, 110–11.

24. Robert E. Lee, *"To Markie": The Letters of Robert E. Lee to Martha Custis Williams*, ed. Avery Craven (Cambridge: Harvard University Press, 1933), 71–72; Lee to Rooney Lee, January 29, 1861, in Rachal, ed., "Secession is Nothing But Revolution," 6.

25. Lee officially transferred Virginia state forces to Confederate service on June 8, 1861 ("General Orders, No. 25, June 8, 1861," in Lee, *Wartime Papers*, 44–45). He was commissioned a brigadier general in the Confederate army on May 14, 1861, and promoted to full general exactly one month later.

26. Lee to Andrew G. McGrath, December 24, 1861, in Lee, *Wartime Papers*, 93–94. For another letter on the same subject, see Lee to Secretary of War Judah P. Benjamin, February 6, 1862, in ibid., 110.

27. Lee to Henry T. Clark, August 8, 1862, in ibid., 248–49.

28. Charles Marshall, *An Aide-De-Camp of Lee: Being the Papers of Colonel Charles Marshall, Sometime Aide-De-Camp, Military Secretary, and Assistant Adjutant General on the Staff of Robert E. Lee, 1862–1865*, ed. Sir Frederick Maurice (Boston: Little, Brown, 1927), 30–32; Mark A. Weitz, *More Damning than Slaughter: Desertion in the Confederate Army* (Lincoln: University of Nebraska Press, 2005), 74–75, 78, 107–8.

29. Marshall, *Aide-De-Camp of Lee*, 30–32; Lee to John Letcher, December 21, 1861, in J. William Jones and others, eds., *Southern Historical Soci-*

ety Papers, 52 vols. (1876–1959; reprint with 3-vol. index, Wilmington, N.C.: Broadfoot, 1990–92), 1:462.

30. William Preston Johnston, "Memoranda of Conversations with General R. E. Lee," in Gallagher, ed., *Lee the Soldier*, 30 (Lee and Johnston met on May 7, 1868); Lee to G. W. C. Lee, in Lee, *Wartime Papers*, 410–11.

31. Lee to Jefferson Davis, January 13, 1864, in Lee, *Wartime Papers*, 650–51.

32. Lee to James L. Kemper, January 29, 1864, Lee to Quartermaster General Alexander R. Lawton, January 19, 1864, Lee to Secretary of War James A. Seddon, April 12, 1864, in ibid., 663, 653, 696.

33. Lee to Jefferson Davis, September 2, 1864, in ibid., 847–49.

34. Lee to Andrew Hunter, January 11, 1865, in U.S. War Department, *The War of the Rebellion: A Compilation of the Official Records of the Union and Confederate Armies*, 127 vols., index, and atlas (Washington: GPO, 1880–1901), ser. 4, vol. 3:1012–13 (hereafter cited as *OR*); Lee to Ethelbert Barksdale, February 18, 1865, in James D. McCabe Jr., *Life and Campaigns of General Robert E. Lee* (Atlanta: National Publishing Company, 1866), 574–75. The letter to Barksdale was released to the newspaper and proved very influential with the public and members of Congress. Lee had made similar arguments in private correspondence with William Porcher Miles of South Carolina in the autumn of 1864. See Robert F. Durden, *The Gray and the Black: The Confederate Debate on Emancipation* (Baton Rouge: Louisiana State University Press, 1972), 135–36.

35. *OR*, ser. 4, vol. 3:1012–13.

36. Edward A. Pollard, *Lee and His Lieutenants; Comprising the Early Life, Public Services, and Campaigns of General Robert E. Lee and His Companions in Arms, with a Record of Their Campaigns and Heroic Deeds* (New York: E. B. Treat, 1867), 119; Robert E. Lee Jr., *Recollections and Letters of General Robert E. Lee* (New York: Doubleday, Page, 1904), 78. Lee's son observed that the incident at Antietam "has been told very often and in many different ways." The version here quoted "is what I [Lee's son] remember of it."

37. Johnston, "Memoranda of Conversations," 32 (Lee and Johnston met on March 18, 1870).

38. On whether the conflict was a "total war," see Mark Grimsley, *The Hard Hand of War: Union Military Policy toward Southern Civilians, 1861–1865* (New York: Cambridge, 1995), and Mark E. Neely Jr., *The Civil War and the Limits of Destruction* (Cambridge, Mass.: Harvard, 2007).

39. Lee to Edward C. Turner, September 14, 1861, item #7959, box 1, Lee Papers, Small Library, UVA; Lee to his daughter Annie, December 8, 1861, in Lee, *Recollections and Letters*, 56–57; Lee to "My Dear Daughter," December 25, 1861, in J. William Jones, *Personal Reminiscences, Anecdotes, and Letters of Gen. Robert E. Lee* (New York: D. Appleton, 1875), 385–86. After learning that thousands of U.S. soldiers were being buried at Arlington, Mary Custis Lee gave free rein to her anger. "They are planted up to the very door," she wrote, "without any regard to common decency" (Pryor, *Reading the Man*,

313). On Custis Lee's suit to gain compensation for the federal government's seizure of Arlington, see Anthony J. Gaughan, *The Last Battle of the Civil War: United States Versus Lee, 1861–1883* (Baton Rouge: Louisiana State University Press, 2011).

40. *OR*, ser. 1, vol. 11, pt. 2:936; John Esten Cooke, *A Life of Gen. Robert E. Lee* (New York: D. Appleton, 1871), 177.

41. Lee to Martha Custis Williams, December 1, 1866, in Lee, *"To Markie"*, 71–72.

42. Lee to Mary Custis Lee, August 14, 1864, in Lee, *Wartime Papers*, 837.

43. Lee to Agnes Lee, May 25, 1863, Lee to Mary Custis Lee, July 7, 1863, in ibid., 492–93, 542.

44. General Orders, No. 61, May 11, 1863, in ibid., 485.

45. William S. Baker, *Itinerary of General Washington from June 15, 1775, to December 23, 1783* (Philadelphia: J. B. Lippincott, 1892), 120–21.

46. "General Orders, No. 75," July 7, 1862, "General Orders, No. 7," January 22, 1864, in Lee, *Wartime Papers*, 210–11, 659.

47. "General Order, No. 9," April 10, 1865, in Lee, *Wartime Papers*, 934–35.

48. Washington's farewell, headed "Rocky Hill, near Princeton, 2 November 1783," is available from the Papers of George Washington project at the University of Virginia at http://gwpapers.virginia.edu/documents/revolution/farewell/index.html (accessed May 30, 2012).

49. Lee to Sir John Dalberg Acton (Lord Acton), December 15, 1866, Lee Family Digital Archive, Washington and Lee University, http://leearchive.wlu.edu/papers/letters/transcripts-unknown%20sources/u021.html (accessed May 29, 2012). For a succinct discussion of the Radical legislation, see James G. Randall and David Donald, *The Civil War and Reconstruction*, 2nd ed. (Lexington, Mass.: D. C. Heath, 1969), chap. 34.

50. Amnesty required an application and a witnessed sworn oath. Lee initially sent in his application without the oath. Secretary of State William Henry Seward pocketed the application and later gave it away as a gift. Lee subsequently sent in a witnessed oath dated October 2, 1865. Because there was no application accompanying the oath, the latter was set aside. The oath was discovered in 1970, at which time Congress granted Lee a return of his full citizenship.

51. Lee to Capt. Josiah Tatnall, September 7, 1865, in Jones, *Life and Letters of Lee*, 387–88; Lee to Jubal A. Early, March 15, 1866, George H. and Katherine M. Davis Collection, Tulane University, New Orleans, La.

52. Lee to Varina Davis, February 23, 1866, in Lee, *Recollections and Letters*, 223–24. Some scholars have challenged Lee's reputation as a postwar conciliator. They typically concede that he publicly called for submission to the North but emphasize his belief in state rights, lack of enthusiasm for the new racial order in the South, and refusal to concede unequivocally that secession was unconstitutional. "Contrary to the Lee tradition," writes Alan T. Nolan, one of the most influential of these scholars, "it appears that after the war the general's attitudes matched those of most of his fellow Southerners in spite of

some conciliatory statements. . . . He was, in brief, a mainstream secessionist after the war, the typical Southern partisan one would expect from his environment and experience" (Nolan, *Lee Considered*, 152).

53. Lee to Thomas L. Rosser, December 13, 1866, item #1171, box 2, Lee Papers, Small Library, UVA. Lee referred to the work of Ladies' Memorial Associations in reburying the Confederate dead. See Caroline E. Janney, *Burying the Dead but Not the Past: Ladies' Memorial Associations and the Lost Cause* (Chapel Hill: University of North Carolina Press, 2007).

Chapter 2. He Died as Became a Confederate Soldier

1. A concise treatment of the sectional controversies that unfolded during Ramseur's formative years is Michael F. Holt, *The Fate of Their Country: Politicians, Slavery Extension, and the Coming of the Civil War* (New York: Hill and Wang, 2004).

2. The next six paragraphs are drawn from Gary W. Gallagher, *Stephen Dodson Ramseur: Lee's Gallant General* (Chapel Hill: University of North Carolina Press, 1985). Only sources for specific quotations are given.

3. Benjamin Sloan to Mary Dodson Ramseur, December 10, 1898, folder 3, Stephen Dodson Ramseur Papers, Southern Historical Collection, University of North Carolina, Chapel Hill (repository hereafter cited as SHC). Sloan was a classmate from South Carolina.

4. U.S. War Department, *The War of the Rebellion: A Compilation of the Official Records of the Union and Confederate Armies*, 127 vols., index, and atlas (Washington: GPO, 1880–1901), ser. 1, vol. 43, pt. 1:553 (Lee), 600 (Grimes) (hereafter cited as *OR*); [E. H. Harding], "Sketch of Major General S. D. Ramseur," *Land We Love* 5 (May 1868): 9; *Raleigh Confederate*, October 28, 1864; Thomas H. Carter to My Precious Wife, October 26, 1864, quoted by permission of Fielding Williams.

5. The family spelled the name Ramsour until Stephen Dodson's father changed the spelling to Ramseur. The precise date and reason for Jacob A. Ramseur's action remain unknown.

6. Stephen Dodson Ramseur (hereafter SDR) to My own dear Mother, September 30, 1855, SDR to David Schenck, August 23, 1855, in Stephen Dodson Ramseur, *The Bravest of the Brave: The Correspondence of Stephen Dodson Ramseur*, ed. George G. Kundahl (Chapel Hill: University of North Carolina Press, 2010), 27, 24.

7. SDR to David Schenck, August 23, 1855, in ibid., 24. For two other letters that discuss politics in North Carolina, see SDR to David Schenck, May 2, [16], 1856, in ibid., 36–38.

8. SDR to My Dear Brother, September 7, 1861, in Ramseur, *Bravest of the Brave*, 78.

9. SDR to My Dear Brother (late August 1863), in ibid., 162.

10. SDR to My Dear Brother, February 16, 1864, in ibid., 198–99. On Holden, the peace movement in North Carolina, and the gubernatorial contest

in 1864, see William C. Harris, *William Woods Holden: Firebrand of North Carolina Politics* (Baton Rouge: Louisiana State University Press, 1987); Paul D. Escott, ed., *North Carolinians in the Era of the Civil War and Reconstruction* (Chapel Hill: University of North Carolina Press, 2008); Gordon B. McKinney, *Zeb Vance: North Carolina's Civil War Governor and Gilded Age Political Leader* (Chapel Hill: University of North Carolina Press, 2004). For the returns in the gubernatorial election, see Harris, *William Woods Holden*, 151–52.

11. SDR to My Own Darling Wife, August 30, 1864, SDR to Dear Brother, [May] 10, 1863, in Ramseur, *Bravest of the Brave*, 260, 132. Ramseur believed his troops had moved through part of the famous Stonewall Brigade during the assault at Chancellorsville, which officers in the Virginia unit hotly denied. On this dispute, see Gallagher, *Stephen Dodson Ramseur*, 61–66; SDR to Col. J. H. S. Funk, May 22, 1863, in Ramseur, *Bravest of the Brave*, 137–38.

12. R. E. Lee to Zebulon B. Vance, June 4, 1863, in OR, ser. 1, vol. 27, pt. 3:871; Ramseur's report, dated May 23, 1863, is in Ramseur, *Bravest of the Brave*, 138–43 (quotation p. 142).

13. SDR to David Schenck, August 23, 1855, in ibid., 21; William L. Sherrill, *Annals of Lincoln County North Carolina: Containing Interesting and Authentic Facts of Lincoln County History Through The Years 1749–1937* (1937; reprint, Baltimore: Regional Publishing Company, 1972), 43, 128; Rodney Steward, *David Schenck and the Contours of Confederate Identity* (Knoxville: University of Tennessee Press, 2012), 1–2.

14. SDR to Luly Ramseur, February 13, 1860, SDR to Ellen Richmond, February 24, 1860, SDR to David Schenck, August 23, 1855, April 6, 1857, in Ramseur, *Bravest of the Brave*, 68, 23, 47.

15. SDR to David Schenck, September 13, 1856, in ibid., 40. On the seismic political impact of the troubles in Kansas, see Nicole Etcheson, *Bleeding Kansas: Contested Liberty in the Civil War Era* (Lawrence: University Press of Kansas, 2004); Robert E. McGlone, *John Brown's War against Slavery* (New York: Cambridge University Press, 2009), chapters 5–6.

16. SDR to David Schenck, November 8, 1856, in Ramseur, *Bravest of the Brave*, 43.

17. Ibid. Anyone interested in exploring whether Ramseur was correct in thinking the antebellum South differed in fundamental ways from the free states will confront a massive and contradictory literature. Two classic titles well worth reading on this topic are Frederick Law Olmsted, *The Cotton Kingdom: A Traveller's Observations on Cotton and Slavery in the American Slave States*, ed. Arthur M. Schlesinger (New York: Knopf, 1953), and Alexis De Tocqueville, *Democracy in America*, trans. Arthur Goldhammer (New York: Library of America, 2004), especially pp. 365–476.

18. SDR to David Schenck, January 24, 1858, in Ramseur, *Bravest of the Brave*, 51–52. For the northern equivalent of Ramseur's concerns about sectional inequality, see Leonard L. Richards, *The Slave Power: The Free North and Southern Domination, 1780–1860* (Baton Rouge: Louisiana State University Press, 2000).

19. SDR to David Schenck, October 27, 1855, January 24, 1858, in Ramseur, *Bravest of the Brave*, 31, 51; Wesley Merritt to Mary Dodson Ramseur, November 8, [?], folder 3, Ramseur Papers, SHC; SDR to David Schenck, April 12, 1856, folder 14, ibid.

20. SDR to David Schenck, October 27, 1855, SDR to Jacob A. Ramseur, August 30, 1855, in Ramseur, *Bravest of the Brave*, 31, 25; SDR to Lucy Dodson Ramseur, August 15, 1855, folder 6, Ramseur Papers, SHC; James Harrison Wilson, *Under the Old Flag*, 2 vols. (New York: D. Appleton, 1912), 1:20–21; Morris Schaff, *The Spirit of Old West Point* (Boston: Houghton Mifflin, 1907), 142–45.

21. SDR to David Schenck, November 8, 1857, in Ramseur, *Bravest of the Brave*, 48–49; Steward, *David Schenck*, 17–18.

22. John G. Barrett, *The Civil War in North Carolina* (Chapel Hill: University of North Carolina Press, 1963), 8–9; Abraham Lincoln, *The Collected Works of Abraham Lincoln*, ed. Roy P. Basler, 9 vols. (New Brunswick, N.J.: Rutgers University Press, 1953–55), 4:271; SDR to David Schenck, September 13, 1856, SDR to Col. L. Thomas, April 5, 1861, in Ramseur, *Bravest of the Brave*, 40, 73. Another young North Carolina officer wrote about the state's failure to move quickly in a way Ramseur would have praised. "I am disgusted with North Carolina," stated William Dorsey Pender on May 4, 1861. If it dragged its feet much longer, "N.C. is a doomed state—either to subjection or eternal disgrace." (William Dorsey Pender, *The General to His Lady: The Civil War Letters of William Dorsey Pender to Fanny Pender*, ed. William W. Hassler [Chapel Hill: University of North Carolina Press, 1965], 18.)

23. Paul Quigley's *Shifting Grounds: Nationalism and the American South, 1848–1865* (New York: Oxford University Press, 2012) is an excellent place to begin an exploration of the topic of nascent southern nationalism. Three older titles that retain value are Jesse T. Carpenter, *The South as a Conscious Minority, 1789–1861: A Study in Political Thought* (1930; reprint, Columbia, University of South Carolina Press, 1990); Avery O. Craven, *The Growth of Southern Nationalism, 1848–1861* (Baton Rouge: Louisiana State University Press, 1953); and John McCardell, *The Idea of a Southern Nation: Southern Nationalists and Southern Nationalism, 1830–1860* (New York: W. W. Norton, 1977). For the centrality of slavery and the desire to maintain racial control among secessionists, see Charles B. Dew, *Apostles of Disunion: Southern Secession Commissioners and the Causes of the Civil War* (Charlottesville: University Press of Virginia, 2001). Elizabeth R. Varon's *Disunion! The Coming of the American Civil War, 1789–1859* (Chapel Hill: University of North Carolina Press, 2008), highlights the impact of abolitionists' thought and actions on the slaveholding South.

24. SDR to David Schenck, September 13, 1856, in Ramseur, *Bravest of the Brave*, 40; Jon L. Wakelyn, ed., *Southern Pamphlets on Secession: November 1860–April 1861* (Chapel Hill: University of North Carolina Press, 1996), 406, 412.

25. For a discussion of the possible the impact of young Confederate officers,

see Gary W. Gallagher, *The Confederate War* (Cambridge, Mass.: Harvard University Press, 1997), 96–110. Jason Phillips, *Diehard Rebels: The Confederate Culture of Invincibility* (Athens: University of Georgia Press, 2007), explores the broader phenomenon of unwavering support for the Confederacy. William W. Freehling's *The South Versus the South: How Anti-Confederate Southerners Shaped the Course of the Civil War* (New York: Oxford University Press, 2001) examines white and black southerners who opposed the Confederacy.

26. SDR to My Darling Wife, December 17, 1863, SDR to My Dear Brother, February 16, 1864, SDR to My Dear Brother, January 28, 1864, in ibid., 191, 199, 195–96.

27. SDR to My Dear Brother, March 11, 1862, in ibid., 86. Ramseur's allusion to a dictator seems extreme, but many Confederates subsequently favored giving Lee such broad power.

28. Paul D. Escott, *Military Necessity: Civil-Military Relations in the Confederacy* (Westport, Conn.: Praeger Security International, 2006), examines debates arising from national mobilization. For a useful collection of testimony from North Carolinians, see W. Buck Yearns and John G. Barrett, eds., *North Carolina Civil War Documentary* (Chapel Hill: University of North Carolina Press, 1980). See also Martin Crawford, *Ashe County's Civil War: Community and Society in the Appalachian South* (Charlottesville: University Press of Virginia, 2001), and Barton A. Myers, *Executing Daniel Bright: Race, Loyalty, and Guerrilla Violence in a Coastal Carolina Community* (Baton Rouge: Louisiana State University Press, 2009).

29. SDR to Ellen Richmond, March 26, 1863, October 5, 1864, in Ramseur, *Bravest of the Brave*, 121, 283.

30. Frank Huger to My Dear Mother, July 8, 1863, typescript of original courtesy of Lloyd Smith, Charlottesville, Virginia; *OR* 25 (1): 886 (Hill), 889 (Stuart); Jubal A. Early, *A Memoir of the Last Year of the War for Independence in the Confederate States of America, Containing an Account of the Operations of His Commands in the Years 1864 and 1865* (1866; reprint, Columbia: University of South Carolina Press, 2001), 118–19; William M. Norman, *A Portion of My Life: Being a Short & Imperfect History Written While a Prisoner of War on Johnson's Island 1864* (Winston-Salem, N.C.: John F. Blair, 1959), 183.

31. SDR to Ellen Richmond, August 3, 1863, SDR to My Own Darling Wife, September 14, 1864, in Ramseur, *Bravest of the Brave*, 157, 273.

32. SDR to Ellen Richmond, March 26, December 15, 1863, SDR to My Own Darling Wife, September 14, 1864, in ibid., 121, 189, 270.

33. SDR to My Precious Wife, April 24, 1864, SDR to My Own Darling Wife, September 7, 1864, in ibid., 209, 265.

34. SDR to My Own Darling Wife, September 7, 1864, in ibid., 266.

35. H. H. Hutchinson to Mrs. S. D. Ramseur, October 20, 1864, in ibid., 292, 294.

1. I first explored some of the themes in this chapter in "From Antebellum Unionist to Lost Cause Warrior: The Personal Journey of Jubal A. Early," in John Y. Simon and Michael E. Stevens, eds., *New Perspectives on the Civil War: Myths and Realities of the National Conflict* (Madison, Wisc.: Madison House, 1998), 93–118. Rowman and Littlefield Publishing Group has since acquired the copyright and graciously granted permission for me to use material from the original essay.

2. George H. Reese, ed., *Proceedings of the Virginia State Convention of 1861*, 4 vols. (Richmond: Virginia State Library, 1965), 3:722–23.

3. Jubal A. Early (hereafter JAE in citing correspondence) to P. G. T. Beauregard, October 30, 1865, in *The Beauregard Papers, Catalogue No. 1148* (Philadelphia: Stan V. Henkels, [1915], 56–57 [item 251]); JAE to Thomas L. Rosser, May 10, 1866, in William D. Hoyt Jr., ed., "New Light on General Jubal A. Early after Appomattox," *Journal of Southern History* 9 (February–November 1943): 113–17; Jubal A. Early, *A Memoir of the Last Year of the War for Independence, in the Confederate States of America, Containing an Account of the Operation of His Commands in the Years 1864 and 1865* (Lynchburg: Charles W. Button, 1867), vi–vii. The first edition of Early's memoir appeared in 1866 from the Toronto printing firm Lovell and Gibson. No other important figure, Union or Confederate, was so quick to publish a reminiscence.

4. Jubal A. Early, "To the Voters of Franklin, Henry & Patrick Counties," July 20, 1850, Scrapbook, Jubal A. Early Papers, Library of Congress, Washington, D.C. (hereafter cited as Early Papers, LC). Early issued this statement of principles while a candidate for delegate to a state constitutional convention.

5. Reese, ed., *Proceedings*, 3:357–59.

6. "1830 Personal Property Tax List, Franklin County, Virginia," *Virginia Appalachian Notes* 8 (February 1984): 4; extracts from Franklin County tax lists supplied to the author by H. L. Hopkins of Rocky Mount, Virginia; R. H. Early, *The Family of Early, Which Settled upon the Eastern Shore of Virginia, and Its Connections with Other Families* (Lynchburg, Va.: Press of Brown-Morrison Co., 1920), 107–8; Everard H. Smith, ed., "The Civil War Diary of Peter W. Hairston, Volunteer Aide to Major General Jubal A. Early, November 7–December 4, 1863," *North Carolina Historical Review* 67 (January 1990): 59; Jubal A. Early, *Lieutenant General Jubal Anderson Early, C.S.A.: Autobiographical Sketch and Narrative of the War between the States* (1912; reprint, Wilmington, N.C.: Broadfoot Publishing Company, 1989), xviii, xx.

7. JAE to Joab Early, November 8, 1835, Scrapbook, Early Papers, LC.

8. Early, *Autobiographical Sketch and Narrative*, xxi–xxiii. See Lee A. Wallace Jr., "The First Regiment of Virginia Volunteers 1846–1848," *Virginia Magazine of History and Biography* 77 (January 1969): 46–77, on Early and the First Virginia during the war with Mexico.

9. Early, *Autobiographical Sketch and Narrative*, xx, xxiv; *Lynchburg Virginian*, May 30, 1853, July 11, 1856, February 7, 12, 1861.

10. The substance of the following six paragraphs is taken from Early's *Autobiographical Sketch and Narrative* and my introduction (i–xxxvii) to the 1989 Broadfoot reprint. Only sources for specific quotations are given.

11. JAE to Richard S. Ewell, James A. Walker Compiled Service Record, microfilm roll 257, National Archives, Washington, D.C. (repository hereafter NA).

12. Gilbert Moxley Sorrel, *Recollections of a Confederate Staff Officer* (1905; reprint, Jackson, Tenn.: McCowet-Mercer, 1958), 238–39.

13. Letter from "Phax," *Mobile Advertiser*, September 15, 1864 (physical description and reference to Lee's nickname for Early); Smith, ed., "Diary of Peter W. Hairston," 66–67. Hairston was Early's cousin. The only other subordinate who received an affectionate nickname from Lee was James Longstreet, whom the army chief called "my old war horse" on the field at Antietam.

14. Early, *Autobiographical Sketch and Narrative*, 468–69 (reproducing Lee's letter to Early, dated March 30, 1865, removing him from command); Sarah Strickler Fife diary, March 7, 1865, p. 46, Albert and Shirley Small Special Collections Library, University of Virginia, Charlottesville (repository hereafter cited as Small Library, UVA).

15. Jubal A. Early, *The Campaigns of Gen. Robert E. Lee. An Address by Lieut. General Jubal A. Early, before Washington and Lee University, January 19th, 1872* (Baltimore: John Murphy, 1872), 52; Early, "To the Voters of Franklin, Henry & Patrick Counties," July 20, 1850, Early Papers, LC; *Lynchburg Virginian*, February 7, 1861.

16. John Lipscomb Johnson, *Autobiographical Notes* ([Boulder, Colo.]: privately printed, 1958), 129; Reese, ed., *Proceedings*, 4:540.

17. Reese, ed., *Proceedings*, 3:724–26.

18. Ibid., 3:287.

19. Ibid., 163 (April 4 vote); 4:144 (April 17 vote), 494 (April 25 vote), 58–60 (Early's comments on April 16).

20. Ibid., 4:362; JAE to John Letcher, May 2, 1861, file "Mar-25–1," folder "E–F," Virginia Historical Society, Richmond (repository hereafter VHS); Early, *Autobiographical Sketch and Narrative*, 1–2.

21. "Virginia's Ordinance of Secession," *Confederate Veteran* 40 (April 1932):128 (reproducing Early's commentary about why he signed the ordinance); Early, *Memoir of Last Year*, iii–iv.

22. Reese, ed., *Proceedings*, 1:428.

23. JAE to William Ballard Preston, January 11, September 14, 1850, Mss 1/P9267/d/418–23, Preston Family Papers, Early-Preston Letters, VHS; Reese, ed., *Proceedings*, 3:358; Jubal A. Early, *The Heritage of the South: A History of the Introduction of Slavery, Its Establishment from Colonial Times and Final Effect Upon the Politics of the United States*, ed. R. H. Early (Lynchburg, Va.: Press of Brown-Morrison Co., 1915), 78. Published by his niece twenty-one years after Early's death, *The Heritage of the South* was written between 1865 and 1870. In an editor's note, Ruth Early noted that the manuscript had "lain unpublished during the passing of half a century, till passion having cooled and prejudice abated, there is no longer reason for clash from

difference of feeling upon the subject." (p. [3].) In a letter to his brother Sam dated June 4, 1868 (Early Papers, LC), Early stated that he was working on the history of "slavery & the slave trade in the United States & of the slavery agitation."

24. *Lynchburg Daily Virginian*, July 11, 1856; Early, *Heritage of the South*, 48, 61.

25. *Lynchburg Daily Virginian*, December 13, 1859.

26. Ibid.

27. Extracts from Franklin County tax lists supplied to the author by H. L. Hopkins of Rocky Mount, Virginia. The relative was Ruth H. Early, whose quotation is from her editor's note in *Heritage of the South*, [p. 7].

28. Early, *Heritage of the South*, 51–52.

29. Jubal A. Early, "Slavery," undated ms., 1–5, 9, 13–15, folder titled "J. A. Early Addresses and Papers," vol. 16, Early Papers, LC. Early almost certainly composed this essay at about the same time he wrote what was eventually published as *The Heritage of the South*. The two overlap in some ways, and both illustrate his interest in slavery as it related to the background and history of the Confederacy.

30. Early, "Slavery," 16–17.

31. Early, *Memoir of the Last Year*, vii–ix.

32. John Warwick Daniel, description of Early's character in folder titled "Introductory Chapter [Notes & Pages of a Rough Draft] I," box 25, John Warwick Daniel Papers, Small Library, UVA; Early, *Heritage of the South*, 92.

33. Early, *Memoir of the Last Year*, iv.

34. JAE to James L. Kemper, February 9, 1862, Ms. 4083, James L. Kemper Papers, Small Library, UVA.

35. JAE to General Samuel Cooper, November 18, 1864, item 838, roll number 148, Letters Received, Adjutant and Inspector General's Office, Confederate States of America, NA.

36. "The Haversack," *Land We Love* 5 (September 1868): 441–42. The staff officer was Henry Kyd Douglas. Various versions of this episode and others like it appear in the literature.

37. JAE to James L. Kemper, February 4, 1862, Ms. 4083, Kemper Papers, Small Library, UVA; James L. Kemper to JAE, February 14, 1862, Early Papers, LC.

38. John B. Gordon, *Reminiscences of the Civil War* (1903; reprint, Dayton, Ohio: Morningside, 1993), 325; "The Haversack," *Land We Love* 2 (January 1867): 222. For a slightly different version of the incident with Breckinridge, see John Warwick Daniel's account in folder titled "Cedar Creek 19 Oct 1864," box 22, John Warwick Daniel Papers, Small Library, UVA. Former Confederate general Daniel Harvey Hill, who edited *Land We Love*, stated that the "clamor about 'the rights in the territories'" was Early's "special abhorrence."

39. Early, *Memoir of the Last Year*, vi–vii; Jubal A. Early, "Diary of Lt. Genl Jubal A. Early. After leaving the state of Virginia subsequent to Genl R. E. Lee's Surrender," (copy), entries for June 21, 24, 1865, Jones Memorial Library,

Lynchburg, Virginia; JAE to Maj. John Claiborne, July 10, 1870, Early Papers, LC.

40. Early, *Autobiographical Sketch and Narrative*, xxii; Martin F. Schmitt, ed., "An Interview with General Jubal A. Early in 1889," *Journal of Southern History* 11 (November 1945): 562.

41. Early, *Memoir of the Last Year*, 48, 50, 73. On the magnitude of Sheridan's destruction, which was substantial but much exaggerated by many Confederates, see William G. Thomas, "Nothing Ought to Astonish Us: Confederate Civilians in the 1864 Shenandoah Valley Campaign," in Gary W. Gallagher, ed., *The Shenandoah Valley Campaign of 1864* (Chapel Hill: University of North Carolina Press, 2006):222–56.

42. JAE to J.[?] Fraise Richard, May 7, 1886, JAE to "the municipal authorities of Chambersburg, Pennsylvania," July 29, 1864, Jubal A. Early Papers, New-York Historical Society, New York City; Early, *Memoir of the Last Year*, 67–70.

43. Joab Early to JAE, August 10, 1861, January 7, 1863, Mss 1/Ea765/b/4–5, Early Family Papers, VHS.

44. JAE to John C. Breckinridge, March 27, 1867. I am indebted to William C. Davis for permission to quote from the original document.

45. Early, *Heritage of the South*, 116; Early, *Memoir of the Last Year*, viii–ix.

46. JAE to Hunter Holmes McGuire, October 30, 1865, Mss1/M1793/a/3–4, Hunter Holmes McGuire Papers, VHS; JAE to Dear Brother, February 7, 1868, July 16, 1867, Early Papers, LC.

47. JAE to Robert E. Lee, November 20, 1868, folder titled "Introductory Chapter [Notes & Pages of a Rough Draft] I," box 25, John Warwick Daniel Papers, Small Library, UVA.

48. JAE to William H. Payne, Mss1/H9267/a/8, Hunton Family Papers, VHS; Schmitt, ed., "Interview with General Jubal A. Early," 549. Crook's diary entry was for January 4, 1890.

49. Schmitt, ed., "Interview with General Jubal A. Early," 551; *Lynchburg Daily Virginian* (quoting the *Richmond Enquirer*), June 18, 1869. On Early as a Lost Cause warrior, see Thomas L. Connelly, *The Marble Man: Robert E. Lee and His Image in American Society* (New York: Knopf, 1977); Gaines M. Foster, *Ghosts of the Confederacy: Defeat, the Lost Cause, and the Emergence of the New South* (New York: Oxford University Press, 1987); and Gary W. Gallagher, *Lee and His Army in Confederate History* (Chapel Hill: University of North Carolina Press, 2001), 255–82. The best biography, though unsatisfying in some respects, is Charles C. Osborne, *Jubal: The Life and Times of General Jubal A. Early, CSA. Defender of the Lost Cause* (Chapel Hill, N.C.: Algonquin Books of Chapel Hill, 1992).

50. John Warwick Daniel, description of Early's character in folder titled "Introductory Chapter [Notes & Pages of a Rough Draft] I," box 25, John Warwick Daniel Papers, UVA.

1. The traditional estimate of Confederate military dead has been 258,000, although scholars always have conceded that the figure is problematic. In "A Census-Based Count of the Civil War Dead," *Civil War History* 57 (December 2011): 307–48, David J. Hacker makes a compelling case for a much higher number. For a discussion of the older estimate, see E. B. Long, *The Civil War Day by Day: An Almanac, 1861–1865* (Garden City, N.Y.: Doubleday, 1971), 711–12.

2. For an example of the argument that restoration came quickly and relatively easily, see Richard E. Beringer, Herman Hattaway, Archer Jones, and William N. Still Jr., *Why the South Lost the Civil War* (Athens: University of Georgia Press, 1986), 421–23. The most powerful statement of triumphant reconciliation is in David W. Blight, *Race and Reunion: The Civil War in American Memory* (Cambridge, Mass.: Harvard University Press, 2001).

3. Violence in the postwar South has inspired a vast literature, too much of which describes it as a continuation of the war by other means. Although brutal and present in every former Confederate state, the violence, including the actions of the Ku Klux Klan, in no way resembled the massive Confederate military effort that placed hundreds of thousands of men in service and sought to establish a nation. For a useful overview, see George C. Rable, *But There Was No Peace: The Role of Violence in the Politics of Reconstruction* (1984; edition with new preface, Athens: University of Georgia Press, 2007). An example of treating violence in the post-Appomattox years as a continuation of the Civil War is Nicholas Lemann, *Redemption: The Last Battle of the Civil War* (New York: Farrar, Straus, and Giroux, 2006).

4. Caroline E. Janney, *Burying the Dead but Not the Past: Ladies' Memorial Associations and the Lost Cause* (Chapel Hill: University of North Carolina Press, 2007), 1–14; Gaines M. Foster, *Ghosts of the Confederacy: Defeat, the Lost Cause, and the Emergence of the New South* (New York: Oxford University Press, 1987), chaps. 3, 9–10; Timothy S. Sedore, *An Illustrated Guide to Virginia's Confederate Monuments* (Carbondale: Southern Illinois University Press, 2011), passim (for examples, with inscriptions, of typical monuments); John M. Coski, *The Confederate Battle Flag: America's Most Embattled Emblem* (Cambridge, Mass.: Harvard University Press, 2005), 79–80; Gary W. Gallagher, *Causes Won, Lost, and Forgotten: How Hollywood and Popular Art Shape What We Know about the Civil War* (Chapel Hill: University of North Carolina Press, 2008), 149–51. On Confederate iconography, see Mark E. Neely Jr., Harold Holzer, and Gabor S. Boritt, *The Confederate Image: Prints of the Lost Cause* (Chapel Hill: University of North Carolina Press, 1987).

5. "Tributes to General Lee," *Southern Magazine* 1 (January 1871): 8, 10, 24.

6. Foster, *Ghosts of the Confederacy*, 91–92, 101–2; Mrs. B. A. C. Emerson, *Historic Southern Monuments: Representative Memorials of the Heroic Dead of the Southern Confederacy* (New York: Neale, 1911), 443; Cynthia

Mills and Pamela H. Simpson, eds., *Monuments to the Lost Cause: Women, Art, and the Landscapes of Southern Memory* (Knoxville: University of Tennessee Press, 2003), 87. For a sampling of monuments to Lee, see Maurine Whorton Redway, *Marks of Lee on Our Land* (San Antonio, Tex.: Naylor, 1972).

7. Foster, *Ghosts of the Confederacy*, 101; Marshall Fishwick, "Virginians on Olympus II. Robert E. Lee: Saviour of the Lost Cause," *Virginia Magazine of History and Biography* 58 (April 1950): 180.

8. Murray H. Nelligan, *Custis-Lee Mansion: The Robert E. Lee Memorial, Virginia*, National Park Service Historical Handbook Series No. 6 (Washington: National Park Service, 1962), 1; [no author], *Robert E. Lee: The Beloved General* (Boston, Mass.: John Hancock Life Insurance Company, 1926), 16. The five stamps appeared in 1937 (Lee and Stonewall Jackson with Stratford Hall in the background), 1949 (Lee and George Washington with Washington and Lee University in the background), 1955 (a bust of Lee), 1970 (Lee with Jackson and Jefferson Davis on the Confederate memorial at Stone Mountain, Ga.), and 1995 (a three-quarter-length portrait of Lee). Pictures of the five stamps are in U.S. Postal Service, *The Postal Service Guide to Stamps*, 23rd edition (Crawfordsville, Ind.: R. R. Donnelley, 1996). On Lee's development as an American hero, see Thomas L. Connelly, *The Marble Man: Robert E. Lee and His Image in American Society* (New York: Knopf, 1977), chaps. 4–6, and Dixon Wector, *The Hero in America: A Chronicle of Hero-Worship* (New York: Scribner's, 1941), chap. 11.

9. Madge C. Kivett, *A Condensed History of Ramseur, North Carolina* (n.p.: n.p., 1975), 3–4; "Present Portrait General Ramseur," *Lincoln County News*, June 12, 1916; James B. Russell, *Address of James B. Russell at the Unveiling of the Monument Erected to the Memory of Major General Stephen D. Ramseur, September 16, 1920, Cedar Creek Battlefield, Near Middletown, Virginia* (n.p.: n.p., [1920]), [6]; Henry A. du Pont, *Address by Colonel du Pont at Unveiling of Monument to Major General Ramseur* (Winterthur, Del.: privately printed, 1920), 14.

10. Mrs. Bryan Wells [Margaret W.] Collier, *Biographies of Representative Women of the South*, 5 vols. (Atlanta: n.p., 1920–circa 1929), 1:56–59; *Confederate Veteran* 30 (September 1922): 323; typescript of a paper read before the Dodson Ramseur Chapter of the United Daughters of the Confederacy by Annie Craige Allison, February 9, 1935, folder 3, Stephen Dodson Ramseur Papers, Southern Historical Collection, University of North Carolina, Chapel Hill.

11. Jubal A. Early, *The Campaigns of Gen. Robert E. Lee. An Address by Lieut. General Jubal A. Early, before Washington and Lee University, January 19th, 1872* (Baltimore: John Murphy, 1872), 45, 40, 44, 46.

12. John Esten Cooke, *Wearing of the Gray: Being Personal Portraits, Scenes, and Adventures of the War* (1867; reprint, Bloomington: Indiana University Press, 1959), 101; resolution from United Confederate Veterans camp in frames 234–35, reel 36, Jedediah Hotchkiss Papers, Library of Congress, Washington, D.C.

Index

Confederacy, 1, 19, 24, 30, 52; birth of, 20; defeat of, 32, 84, 107n1; diplomatic recognition of, 79–80; domestic chaos in, 79; as godly commonwealth, 28–29

Confederate Congress, 23, 24, 97n34

Confederate government, 23, 52; and conscription, 22; Davis administration of, 2, 40, 74; and impressment, 24; intrusion of, 23

Confederate Memorial Day, 85

Confederate upcountry, 52

Confederate Veteran, 89

Confederate war effort, 21

Confederates, 18, 20, 21, 24, 25–26, 58, 64, 72, 73, 74; commemoration of, 49; defined, 2; identity of, 91; postwar, 84; waging war, 49

Connelly, Thomas L., 10

Conscription, 21–22, 23–24

Continental Army, 3, 29–30, 31

Continental Congress, 29

Cooke, John Esten, 90–91

Cooper, Samuel, 18, 75

"Cornerstone Speech" (Stephens), 50

Craige, Burton, 39

Crook, George, 81

Culpeper Court House, Va., 28

Custer, George Armstrong, 46

Danville, Va., 38

Davidson College, 35, 43

Davis, Jefferson, 23, 25, 29, 50–51, 86; heading new government, 11; usurping power, 22

Davis, Varina, 33

Davis administration, 2, 40, 74

Deep South, 11, 20, 69

Delaware, 2

Democrats, 38, 39, 44, 59–60

Dodson, Lucy Mayfield, 38–39

Dodson, Stephen, 39

Don Quixote (Cervantes), 79–80

Drum, Simon Henry, 19

Du Pont, Henry A., 89

Duty, 5, 28, 32, 73. *See also* Honor

Early, Joab, 60, 65, 78–79

Early, Jubal Anderson, 4, 33, 37, 38, 53, 57–82 passim, 103n4; on African American political class, 80–81; age of, 4, 6; allegiance of, 65–66; as antebellum southerner, 73; in Army of Northern Virginia, 62–64; and Association of the Army of Northern Virginia, 81; in Canada, 80–81, 90; and Civil War memory, 89–90; Civil War service of, 73–80; and Confederate nation, 58, 70, 74, 81–82, 89, 90, 105n29; and Confederates, 64, 77–78; and conscription, 74–75; as conservative, 69; and Constitution, U.S., 73; death of, 90–91; 1872 Address of, 90; in 1860, 4–5; and emancipation, 7, 79, 81; and geography, 69; and Grant, 82; and Lee, 62–63, 81, 90; and Lost Cause, 83; and Louisiana Lottery, 81; loyalties of, 57–58, 73, 82, 90–91; in Lynchburg, 80–82; *Memoir of the Last Year*, 58, 103n3; in Mexico, 59, 68; in minority, 59, 68; and nation, 68, 77, 80, 83; and northerners, 69; patriotic submission of, 60, 67; personal philosophy of, 60; pessimism of, 80–81; political philosophy of, 58–59; in politics, 61, 64; race, 71, 73; and reconciliation, 89–90; and religion, 71; and rights in territories, 76, 105n38; on secession, 66–68, 73, 75–76; on slavery, 70–73, 105n23, 105n29; and Southern Historical Society, 81; and state loyalty, 64, 73, 82; and Texas Revolution, 60–61; and Union, 66–67, 68; and Unionists,

76; and U.S. Army, 77; at Virginia State Convention, 65; and Whig Party, 59, 61–62

Early, Ruth Hairston, 60, 104–5n23, 105n27

Early, Sam, 80

Early family, as slaveholders, 60, 65, 70–71

Economics, 65; Confederate structure of, and slavery, 79

Elections, 61; 1844 presidential, 61; 1850 Virginia State Convention, 103n3; 1856 presidential, 5, 16, 44–45, 61–62; 1860 presidential, 4, 11, 49; 1861 North Carolina State Convention, 48; 1861 Virginia State Convention, 65; 1864 North Carolina gubernatorial, 41, 99–100n10; 1868 Alabama State, 80

Emancipation, 17–18, 25, 52, 71, 72, 78–80, 84, 85

Emancipation Proclamation of 1863, 7, 19, 25, 26–27, 54, 78–79, 96n23

Enlistment (conscription), 21–22, 23–24

Eutaw Springs, battle of, 43

Everett, Edward, 17

Ewell, Richard S., 62

Ex-Confederates, 84–85, 90

Faith. *See* Religion

Federalism, 15–16

Fillmore, Millard, 61–62, 69

Fire-eaters, 17, 68. *See also* Secessionists

First Bull Run, battle of, 62

Fisher's Hill, battle of, 37, 63

Fishwick, Marshall W., 87

Fitzhugh, George, 17

Florida, 46, 86

Floyd, John B., 51

Fort Clinton, N.Y., 43–44

Fort Donelson, Tenn., 51

Fort Sumter, S.C., 11–12, 57–58, 66

Franklin Co., Va., 60

Fredericksburg, Va., 23, 27–28, 62

Free Soilers, 68

Freeman, Douglas Southall, 9–10

Frémont, John C., 44, 45

General Orders, No.1, 13; No. 9, 30–31; No. 61, 29

Generational views, 6, 87, 94n9

Georgia, 26

Gettysburg (film), 10–11

Gettysburg, battle of, 29, 37, 40, 53, 54, 62

Gibbes, Wade Hampton, 47

Gods and Generals (film), 11

Goldfield, David, 10

Gordon, John B., 90

Grant, Ulysses S., 30–31, 51, 63, 82, 87

Greensboro, N.C., 88

Grimes, Bryan, 38

Habeas corpus, Confederate suspension of (1864), 50–51

Hairston, Peter W., 104n13

Hairston, Samuel, 60

Hancock, Winfield Scott, 41

Harpers Ferry, W.Va., 7, 18, 70

Harrison, William Henry, 59

Harrisonburg, Va., 77

Henry, Patrick, 87

Hill, Ambrose Powell, 41, 53, 62

Hill, Daniel Harvey, 105n38

History, U.S., 1–2, 3–4, 7, 9–10, 45–46, 49, 83, 91; on Confederate nation, 83, 84; on conflicting cultures, 45–46; on Lee, 96n23, 98–99n50; and memory, 89

Holden, William Woods, 40–41, 99n10

Honor, 5, 19–20, 57, 73, 93n8. *See also* Duty; Lee, Robert E.; Ramseur, Stephen Dodson

Hooker, Joseph, 62

Nation, 2, 3–4, 6, 15, 49, 50,
52, 55, 93nn2–3, 101n23; as
community, 49–50; Confederate,
1–2, 4, 20, 29, 30, 31, 35, 49,
58, 80, 88, 91, 101–2n25; and
Early, 74; identity of, 1, 33–34,
49, 77, 89; new, 52; rhetoric
of, 53; sentiment of, 74, 83, 84,
93n3. *See also* Confederacy;
Early, Jubal Anderson; Identity;
Lee, Robert E.; Loyalty; Ramseur,
Stephen Dodson
National Park Service, 88
New England, 18–19, 47
New Hampshire, 45
New Mexico Territory, 68, 69
New Orleans, La., 86
New York, 46, 47
Newton, John, 28
Nolan, Alan T., 98–99n52
North, the, 18, 26, 77
North Carolina, 1, 21, 35, 38–42,
51, 52, 88–89, peace movement
in, 99n10; politics in, 39–40;
secession of, 36, 40, 101n22
North Carolina Historical
Commission, 88
North Carolina Standard, 40
North Carolina State Convention, 40
North Carolina Supreme Court, 88
Northerners, 6, 17, 18–19, 44,
46–47, 74, 79, 84

Oath of allegiance, 32
Oberlin College, 47
Ohio, 7, 46, 65
Ordinance of secession (Va.), 67
Overland Campaign, 54

Patriotic submission, 59–60, 74.
See also Early, Jubal Anderson
Patriotism, 5
Pennsylvania, 38, 44, 65, 78
Phillips, Ulrich Bonnell, 7

Pillow, Gideon J., 51
Pittsylvania County, Va., 60
Polk, James K., 15
Pope, John, 27
Popular culture, 10–11
Popular sovereignty, 68–69
Post–Civil War era, 7, 30–33;
Confederate community during,
83–85
Pottawatomie Creek Massacre,
Kans., 44–45
Potter, David M., 3–4, 83

R. E. Lee: A Biography (Freeman),
9–10
Race, 2, 6–7, 73, 80; conflict, 18, 19;
control, 7, 17, 19, 26, 35, 49, 77,
78, 79, 82, 85, 101n23; and Jim
Crow, 79, 85; and Lee, 24–25, 26,
32; and white supremacy, 7, 8, 18,
20, 25, 35, 49, 50, 55, 70–71, 73,
78, 81, 82, 85
Railroads, 24
Raleigh Confederate, 38
Ramseur, Ellen Richmond (Nellie),
37, 52–53, 54–56, 89
Ramseur, Jacob A., 35, 47–48
Ramseur, Lucy Mayfield Dodson, 38;
decline and death of, 48
Ramseur, Mary Dodson, 37, 88–89;
UCV honors, as "Sponsor of the
South," 89
Ramseur, N.C., 88
Ramseur, Stephen Dodson, 1, 4, 18,
35–56 passim, 69, 73, 80; age of,
4, 6; allegiance of, 88; and Army
of Northern Virginia, 41; birth
and background of, 35–36; as
brigade commander, 36–37; and
Buchanan's victory, 45; career of,
43; on Confederate government,
50; Confederate purpose of, 35;
and conflicting cultures, 45–46;
and conscription, 50–51; death of,

37–38, 46, 53, 55–56; as division
commander, 37; in 1860, 4; and
emancipation, 7; and financial
crisis, 48; and home front, 51–52;
and honor, 42; on Lee, 102n27;
loyalties of, 44, 49, 56; marriage
of, 37, 52–53; and memory, 83,
88–89; and military failures, 51;
and mobilization, 51, 52; and
nation, 42, 44, 47, 49, 50, 52–54,
83; on northerners, 45, 46–47,
48, 50; politics of, 39–40, 51–52;
recklessness of, 53; and religion,
55; resolution of, 54–55; and
Revolutionary War, 43–44; on
secession, 40, 45, 46; and slavery,
7, 44; and southern identity, 35,
44, 100n17; and state, 39, 40–42;
and Union, 42–43; in U.S. Army,
36, 48–49; in Washington City, 48
Ramseur family, 38–39; financial
crisis of, 47–48
Ramsour's Mill, battle of, 43, 52
Randolph, George Wythe, 27
Rapidan River, Va., 30, 41, 53
Rappahannock Bridge, battle of, 62
Rappahannock River, Va., 11, 27
Ream's Station, battle of, 41
Reconciliation, 6, 94n10; defined,
84–85; reunion without, 84;
sincere, 89; situational, 32–33,
89–90; triumphalist, 107n2
Reconstruction, 32, 84; violence in,
107n4
Religion, 4–6, 55, 71–72; and military
morale, 29; and nation, 29
Republicans, 44–45, 48, 49, 82;
congressional, 27; radical, 32, 78
Reunion, 84–85. See also
Reconciliation
Revolution, American, 3, 48, 49, 55,
59, 68, 71
Revolutionary War, 14, 29–30,
42–44, 48, 52

Richmond, Ellen (Nellie). See
Ramseur, Ellen Richmond
Richmond, Va., 13, 34, 38, 86–87,
89, 90
Roanoke (Big Lick), Va., 65
Roanoke Island, N.C., 51
Rockingham County, Va., 75
Rocky Mount, Va., 4–5, 60, 64,
70, 73
Rodes, Robert E., 36, 80
Rosser, Thomas L., 81

Santa Anna, 61, 67
Schenck, David, 39–40, 48, 49–50,
52, 101n21
Scott, Winfield, 11–12, 12–13, 16,
17; Mexican campaign of, 15; as
Unionist, 76–77
Secession, 1, 4, 11, 20, 65–68, 80, 84;
constitutionality of, 85, 98n52;
Early's opposition to, 5, 57–58,
65–67, 71; Lee's reaction to, 10,
16–17; Ramseur's support for, 35,
36, 40, 44, 45
Secessionists, 60, 74, 101n23; and
Early, 105n38; as fire-eaters, 17, 68
Sectionalism, 6, 46, 49, 99n1
Seddon, James A., 19, 25, 96n23
Seminole War, 60
Sentiment. See Identity
Seven Days battles, 30
Shaara, Michael, 10
Shenandoah Valley, 26, 37, 63–64,
77, 87, 106n41; 1864 campaign
in, 53, 54
Sheridan, Philip Henry, 26, 38, 63,
64, 77, 106n41
Sherman, William Tecumseh, 26
Slaveholding society, 4, 6, 7, 20,
44, 50, 54, 70, 77, 83, 84; as
civilization, 55; and emancipation,
84; and racial control, 17, 49,
79, 81. See also Race: and white
supremacy

Selected books from the Mercer University Lamar Memorial Lectures

※

The Brown *Decision, Jim Crow, and Southern Identity*
James C. Cobb

Teaching Equality: Black Schools in the Age of Jim Crow
Adam Fairclough

Becoming Confederates: Paths to a New National Loyalty
Gary W. Gallagher

*A Consuming Fire: The Fall of the Confederacy
in the Mind of the White Christian South*
Eugene D. Genovese

Moses, Jesus, and the Trickster in the Evangelical South
Paul Harvey

George Washington and the American Military Tradition
Don Higginbotham

South to the Future: An American Region in the Twenty-First Century
Edited by Fred Hobson

The Countercultural South
Jack Temple Kirby

*Singing Cowboys and Musical Mountaineers:
Southern Culture and the Roots of Country Music*
Bill C. Malone

"Mixed Blood" Indians: Racial Construction in the Early South
Theda Perdue

Camille, 1969: Histories of a Hurricane
Mark M. Smith

Weathering the Storm: Inside Winslow Homer's Gulf Stream
Peter H. Wood